The Taiwan-China Connection

Transitions: Asia and Asian America
Series Editor, *Mark Selden*

The Taiwan-China Connection

Democracy and Development Across the Taiwan Straits

Tse-Kang Leng

冷 則 剛

WestviewPress

A Division of HarperCollins*Publishers*

Transitions: Asia and Asian America

Copyright © 1996 by Westview Press, A Division of HarperCollins Publishers, Inc.

Published in 1996 in the United States of America by Westview Press, 5500 Central Avenue, Boulder, Colorado 80301-2877, and in the United Kingdom by Westview Press, 12 Hid's Copse Road, Cumnor Hill, Oxford OX2 9JJ

Library of Congress Cataloging-in-Publication Data
Leng, Tse-Kang.
  The Taiwan-China connection : democracy and development across the
Taiwan Straits / Tse-Kang Leng.
    p. cm.—(Transitions—Asia and Asian America)
  Includes bibliographical references and index.
  ISBN 0-8133-2982-5.—ISBN 0-8133-9006-0 (pbk.)
  1. Taiwan—Economic policy—1975– 2. Taiwan—Politics and
government—1988– 3. Taiwan—Foreign economic relations—China.
4. China—Foreign economic relations—Taiwan.   I. Title.
II. Series.
HC430.5.L453   1996
338.95124′9—dc20   96-8991
                                                                          CIP

10   9   8   7   6   5   4   3   2 ·   1

To my parents

Contents

Tables and Figures

Acknowledgments

This book is based on my Ph.D. dissertation, submitted to the University of Virginia (UVA) in 1995. I am indebted to many individuals at every stage of work on the manuscript. Special thanks go to Professor Brantly Womack, my dissertation advisor, for his guidance and encouragement. Ever patient and ready to share his insights, Professor Womack guided me into the academic world and taught me how to be a true "scholar." Professor and Mrs. Shao-chuan Leng, my foremost *laoshi* and *shimu*, gave me all the help I needed as a foreign student in the United States. Their character and generosity provided me with a true role model. Professor Kenneth W. Thompson, my mentor in theories of international relations, also provided me with endless support during the years I spent at UVA. Professor John Shepherd, a brilliant anthropologist, gave me insight into an area other than my own subject of political science.

I am also grateful to the friends I made during my four years of study at UVA. I owe a special debt to Mr. and Mrs. John Flachmeyer, my family hosts in Charlottesville. Mr. Flachmeyer carefully read the original draft and corrected the grammatical errors. Mrs. Flachmeyer, sadly, passed away two months after we left the "uplands," but my wife and I will always cherish the memory of her warm hospitality. Miss Chung-ming Lung of the East Asian Division of the Alderman Library was kind enough to offer me a part-time job when my finances became strained. Another friend in Charlottesville I am particularly grateful to is Mr. Charlie Chihpin Tu.

In Taiwan, many thanks go to Professor Milton D. Yeh and Dr. Yujen Chou, who have given me many valuable suggestions since I started preparing this book. My teachers at National Chengchi University, including Professor Yu-hsien Long, Bih-jaw Lin, Kuo-hsiung Lee, Chi Su, I-chou Liu, and Jyh-pin Fa provided me with very useful advice and encouragement. My appreciation also goes to Ms. Judith Fletcher of the Institute of International Relations, who has kindly proofread and revised the prose of the original draft under the pressure of an approaching submission date.

In addition, I am pleased to record my very special thanks to Professor Mark Selden, the series editor, for his comments on the original manuscript. This book would not have been published without his insightful suggestions and recommendations. I would also like to thank Susan McEachern and Melanie Stafford at Westview Press for their assistance during the preparation of the book. Needless to say, despite the generous assistance I have received, I remain responsible for all the opinions I put forward.

This book is dedicated to my parents. They rebuilt a family in Taiwan during the island's most impoverished years and struggled to help their children receive the highest education possible in the United States. Without their material and spiritual support, I would never have been able to complete my studies and write this book.

Finally, I am deeply indebted to my wife, Wenshan, whose boundless devotion and assistance encouraged me to achieve our common goals.

Tse-Kang Leng
Taipei, Taiwan

1

Introduction

Students of comparative politics and international relations will find the recent development of Taiwan an interesting case to test the validity of competing theories of social science. On the one hand, the process of democratization and the transformation of state-society relations challenge the "strong-state paradigm" that has been used to explain the political economy of Taiwan; on the other, Taiwan's flourishing relationship with China[1] requires a new theoretical framework for foreign policy analysis.

The strong-state paradigm is a powerful tool for explaining Taiwan's development over the past forty-some years. Although the neoliberal school of political economy stresses the advantage of laissez-faire policies and dependency theorists emphasize international constraints upon development, the focus of the statist approach is the state's capacity and its autonomy in manipulating the state-society relationship and in initiating foreign economic policies. However, since the process of democratization began, the strong state's dominant role in policymaking has been reduced. Academic works discussing the transitional role of the strong state in initiating economic policies are rare.

This book focuses on the changing nature of the state in Taiwan and the making of its economic policy toward China. The case of Taiwan-China economic relations is selected because it is highly political and vital to Taiwan's survival. This special kind of relationship reflects the domestic power constellation in Taiwan and has produced conflicts within the bureaucratic hierarchy and general public. Discussing the management of economic transactions across the Taiwan Straits can help us understand changing state capacity, state autonomy, and state-society relations in the democratization era.

The Failure of State Intervention in
Cross-Straits Economic Relations

Taiwan's economic development over the past forty years is commonly characterized as state-led growth coupled with a fairly equal distribution of wealth. In the early stage of development, the state supported infant industries and established state-owned enterprises to achieve its economic goal of import substitution. In the take-off period of the 1960s and 1970s, the state promoted export-led growth. The state led and controlled the market mechanism by providing tax breaks, subsidizing strategic industries, and regulating business activities. The ultimate goal of the state was to achieve high economic growth through export-oriented small and medium-sized firms concentrated in labor-intensive industries.

State intervention in the authoritarian era was successful. The economic bureaucracy, controlled by Western-trained technocrats, was an efficient and coherent body. Under the authoritarian rule first of the supreme leader Chiang Kai-shek (1886–1975) and then his son Chiang Ching-kuo (1910–1988), the state suppressed any potential opposition forces and dominated the society. Domestic capitalists were divided after the February 28 Massacre of 1947. They began to ally with state officials and state enterprises and to develop a patron-client relationship with the state. Foreign economic policies, used as a tool to promote exports, were the outcome of autonomous state actions initiated by technocrats insulated from the penetration of social interests.

However, the three important factors contributing to the success of intervention by the strong Taiwanese state—a coherent body of technocrats, state dominance over society, and effective state control of business activities—gradually disappeared in the late 1980s, a time of transition in Taiwan. Along with the large-scale political reform, a new relationship with China began to emerge. Although official political contacts between the two sides are still prohibited, interaction in culture, sports, communications, and business has become closer over the past five years.

The Taiwanese government insists on indirect economic transactions with China. However, those sectors of the bureaucracies responsible for economic policies toward China have failed to coordinate the speed, form, and content of cross-Straits economic interaction. Political struggle and factional conflicts in the higher echelons of the ruling party and the state greatly impede cooperation and coordination among the political elite. The result is inconsistency and delay in initiating policies that are aimed at regulating business activities.

Taiwan's economic policy toward China is also influenced by the corporate interests of business groups. As big business groups begin to invest in China, they are using various means to forge both formal and informal alliances with state bureaucrats at home to guarantee their business interests. On the other hand, small and medium-sized firms are rushing into the booming China market regardless of the state prohibition. Restrictive laws and macroeconomic policies have proved ineffective in regulating the activities of businesspeople eager for profit. The incompetent state bureaucracy, divided by factional and elite conflicts, is powerless to resist pressures from society and thus has failed to lead the market interests. The state has only partially legitimized the current situation of economic interaction with China. This is in sharp contrast to the state's dominant role in economic policymaking during Taiwan's authoritarian era.

Cross-Straits Economic Policy as a Case Study

The primary aim of this book is to explain the failure of the Taiwanese state's intervention in cross-Straits economic policy. It does not merely concern itself with the content of the policy but focuses on the policymaking process and state-society interaction on the issue of managing cross-Straits economic relations. The questions we will ask include: How does democratization influence elite coherence and the state-society relationship in Taiwan? What are the major controversies concerning the tempo and form of cross-Straits economic interaction? Why have the various sectors of the state bureaucracy failed to coordinate their policies? What influence does society, especially big business, exert on state policy? What is the real situation of cross-Straits economic interaction? To what degree has the state failed to discourage Taiwan businesses from entering the China market? How do Taiwanese businesspeople avoid legal restrictions and resist state intervention? What is the capacity of the state to regulate the market?

The strongest case studies start out with clearly identified theories that are expected to explain the event. This research challenges the strong-state paradigm, which dominates the study of Taiwan's political economy. By analyzing state autonomy and state capacities, a new form of state-society interaction in the democratization era can be identified. Moreover, this research will not merely analyze the inability of the Taiwanese state to implement a coherent economic policy toward China but will also attempt to identify the major actors and social interests involved in the policymaking process. The aim is to provide at least a partial answer to the broader question of the ability of the state to cooperate with society and achieve major changes in contemporary Taiwan.

The case study used in this research is an empirical one. As Robert Yin argues, a case study is an empirical inquiry that investigates a contemporary phenomenon within its real-life context, and in which multiple sources of evidence are used.[2] The data in this book come from the following categories of sources: (1) *theoretical works:* this study begins with a discussion of existing literature on state theories, the developmental state, and economic development in Taiwan; (2) *official documents:* this includes speeches and other statements of government officials, internal policy documents, official policy statements, and statistical data released by various branches of the government; (3) *newspapers and journals:* this category consists of articles from major newspapers and magazines in Taiwan representing different views and opinions regarding cross-Straits interaction, and statistical data compiled by private research institutes; (4) *interviews:* this important source includes interviews with policymakers, opposition leaders, Taiwanese businesspeople, officials in semigovernmental organizations, and scholars.

Historical and comparative approaches will be used to gain an insight into state-society interaction in Taiwan's policymaking with regard to economic links with China. By focusing on moments of significant structural change, we can determine how economic relationships and the social structure that underlies them come into being as a result of human activity and how they can be transformed through social action.[3] Hence, a comparison will be attempted between the policymaking process in the authoritarian era and that since the beginning of democratization. This historical approach will help us understand the state-society relationship and the evolution of the Taiwanese state.

Theoretical Framework

Taiwan's trade and investment policies toward China constitute a unique form of economic policy. Both sides of the Taiwan Straits deny that cross-Straits economic relations are "international" in nature. Although Taiwan's economic policy toward China is essentially a part of its "foreign" economic policy, it also reflects the domestic political and economic transition of the past few years. Theories of comparative politics and international relations can be used to analyze the policymaking process with regard to cross-Straits economic transactions.

There are three dominant schools of thought that seek to explain international economic policymaking.[4] System-oriented theories stress the international constraints on individual states. From this perspective, a nation-state's position in the international economy decisively shapes its economic policy. Through the establishment of an "international regime" and some functional arrangements, interdependence in international society may produce a spill-over effect and exert an influence on realist state policies. World system theorists explain economic policy as a function of the process and contradiction within international capitalism. Neodependency theorists focus on the "triple alliance"—of transitional capital, local capital, and the entrepreneur in state capitalism—in shaping the bureaucratic-authoritarian state and policy output. System-oriented theories hold that international-level analysis is essential for the effective comparative study of economic policymaking.

The second school of thought, the society-oriented approach, is based on the tradition of individualism and pluralism. Classical theorists of this approach emphasize the importance of interest groups in shaping state policies. In their view, policy results on any particular issue are a function of the varying ability of groups to organize and give their interests prominence in the policy process. Government institutions essentially provide an arena for group competition and do not exert any significant impact on the decisions that emerge.

Proponents of state-oriented economic policy analysis argue that it is necessary to focus on state autonomy and the capacity of the state to participate in the formation of the political setup and the policymaking process. According to this approach, the state should be regarded as an actor, and politicians and administrators are independent participants in the policy process. The state is an organizational institution that shapes individual and group interests. This book adopts a state-centered approach to the study of Taiwan's cross-Straits economic policy.

The State as the Focus of Study

The new trend in state-centered analysis continues the Weberian perspective on the state. Max Weber defined the state as "a human community that claims the monopoly of legitimate use of physical force within a given territory."[5] Administrative, legal, executive, and coercive organizations are the core of the state. Weber's "ideal type" of legitimate force is the bureaucracy. Among Weber's three types of domination, the bureaucracy is the purest type of legal authority. The characteristics of bureaucracy—consistence, calculability, and predictability—are the concretion of Weber's concerns of rationality.[6]

One important issue in defining the "state" is whether it equals the "government." Skocpol and Stepan both adopt the Weberian conceptualization of the state. For Skocpol, the state is a set of administrative, policing, and military organizations headed, and more or less well-coordinated by, an executive authority.[7] While Skocpol focuses on the executive aspect of the state, Stepan argues that the state must be considered as something more than the "government." It is the continuous administrative, legal, bureaucratic, and coercive system that attempts to structure not only the relationship between civil society and public authority in a polity but also many crucial relationships within civil society.[8] In Stepan's explanation, the state is not just a static collection of politicians and regulations. It is a dynamic intruding force influencing and shaping the content of politics in the regime.

By the same token, O'Donnell argues that it is a mistake to equate the state with the state apparatus, the public sector, or the aggregation of public bureaucracies. These are part of the state, not all of it. The state is also, and no less primarily, a set of social relations that establishes a certain order, and ultimately backs it with a centralized coercive guarantee, over a given territory. Many of these relations are formalized in a legal system created and backed by the state. The legal system is a constitutive dimension of the state and the order that it establishes and guarantees over a given territory. That order is based on the principle of "equality," which varies according to the different ideologies the state adopts.[9]

In brief, the "state" is a set of social relations formulated by means of the legal system. The statist approach focuses not only on formal rules and organizations but also on informal routines and procedure. Moreover, these formal and informal rules are put into a larger context of social-economic situations when we are discussing the capacity and institutional goals of state actions. For instance, in his study of American judicial politics, Rosenberg argues that the Supreme Court as a state institution sometimes fails to bring about social changes through its interpretation of the Constitution. It is the interaction of different social forces, rather than the Court's decisions alone, that shifts social trends. These social forces include political leadership, political culture, and local interest groups.[10] All in all, the main difference between the traditional legal approach and the new statist approach in studying politics is that the latter adopts more "interactive" perspectives on state capacity and state autonomy and focuses on the bargaining process between the state and major social forces.

State Autonomy and State Capacities

The statist approach to political studies does not treat the state as a separate unit of analysis. Instead, it puts the state in a larger context of state-society interaction. It analyzes not only the state's autonomy in resisting social influences but also the state's capacity to penetrate into society. Policymaking issues include, first, the state as an actor in realizing policy goals and, second, the impact of the state on the content and working of politics. In other words, the state-centered approach treats the state as an actor in the political and economic game and focuses on politicians and administrators in the executive branch as independent participants in the policy process.

From the statist perspective, the state is not just an arena in which socioeconomic struggles are fought out. It is a macrostructure for social transformation.[11] The conception of state autonomy as freedom from "external" influences relates to a conception of the state "exerting leverage" or "winning out" over the pressures emanating from society. The basic idea is that state leaders have their own ends while social interest groups have theirs. In the political battle that ensues, state leaders resist pressures from private interests and translate their will into public policies.[12] In brief, the term "state autonomy" has been identified with two things: first, with a distinctive state agenda, one not simply derived from the private interests of particular persons in society; and second, with the capacity of the state to pursue and execute its will. State autonomy entails competence in forming objectives and bringing about desired effects.

The state-centered literature considers how the institutional characteristic of the state influences the policy process, particularly the ability of state officials to formulate and implement economic policy. States differ in the extent to which they and their societies are centralized and in the range of policy instruments available to state officials to conduct economic policy. They also differ in the degree of autonomy that state officials enjoy relative to social forces. Given differences in these characteristics, different states can be placed along a continuum that ranges from "weak" to "strong" in relation to their own societies.[13]

According to the state's relation to society, Krasner classifies the state into three categories: the weak state, the moderate state, and the strong state. The "weak state" may be able to resist social pressures, but it cannot change the behavior of the private sector. Central decisionmakers may be able to ignore appeals from large corporations, but they cannot make corporations follow policies that will further the state's goals or create alternative institutions such as state-owned enterprises.

The "moderate state" is able to resist private pressures and persuade private groups to follow policies that are perceived as furthering the national interest, but it cannot impose structural transformation on the domestic environment. The state must work with existing social structures. In economic affairs these structures can be defined in terms of the juridical nature of the institutions controlling economic activities, the distribution of activity among sectors, and the place of particular firms within sectors.

As to the "strong state," it has the power to change the behavior of existing private actors and also, over a period of time, to change the economic structure itself. This state can create new kinds of economic actors. It can build up certain sectors of the economy through credits, tax relief, or other forms of support. It can favor companies whose activities are perceived as serving the national interest.[14]

To sum up, the state-centered approach is not a static perspective. It is also not a state-only perspective of political studies. By analyzing the relationship between state and society, we can gain an understanding of state capacities and state autonomy in the policymaking process. The state-centered approach is appropriate in discussing economic policymaking in countries that have a strong state apparatus and are now in the transitional period of adjusting the state-society relationship.

The "Developmental State" and East Asian Development Model

Since the early 1980s, students of political and economic development have been exploring the role of the "developmental state" in East Asia's export-led growth. The "regulatory state" in Western capitalist countries refrains from interfering in the marketplace except to ensure certain limited goals. In contrast, the developmental states themselves lead the industrialization drive and set up substantive social and economic goals.[15]

The mighty Ministry of International Trade and Industry (MITI) of Japan provides a classic example of a developmental state. As Johnson argues, industrial policies and bureaucratic initiatives in Japan were not completely constrained by political interventions from the Liberal Democratic Party (LDP). Instead, they were insulated from corporate interests. MITI could decide what to import, could establish a foreign exchange budget to promote exports, and could grant licenses for imports and exports. The Supreme Export Council set up export targets for the coming year and offered tax breaks to stimulate exports. Furthermore, MITI could organize cartels through special Industrial Laws, and these cartels could pursue high profits and maintain these profits during a recession. More important, MITI had indicative powers to choose strategic industries for the purpose of economic development. These strategic industries were qualified to apply for special loans from government-owned banks (especially the Japan Development Bank). Hence, in the case of Japan, the state intervened positively to promote export development through strategic industries. The state and state institutions manipulated and governed the market and played crucial roles in Japan's export-led growth.[16]

Taiwan and South Korea provide two more examples of the developmental state. In Taiwan, three important sectors of society—agriculture, labor, and business—had put minimal constraints on the state. Land reform in Taiwan not only equalized income distribution but also created support for the government in rural areas. The Kuomintang (KMT) party-state also put down the labor movement. With the establishment of state-owned enterprises and the subordination of local capitalists, the state developed a patron-client network within the business community.[17] A similar situation existed in South Korea. Land reform and the presence of a strong military ruling elite silenced the union movement and peasant opposition. The military undertook wide-ranging economic reforms. The broad power of the military was important not only in restricting the government but in controlling the opposition. In brief, the strong states in Taiwan and South Korea enjoyed a large degree of "autonomy" in the authoritarian era, significantly more than their Latin American counterparts.[18]

In South Korea, the combination of a growth-oriented centralized economic bureaucracy and a historically shaped political alliance among the military elite, state technocrats, and big business accentuated economic nationalism and gave the national economy an organized competitive advantage in the international economy. Large business groups were organized around state-controlled banks. The state coordinated the export drive through about ten state-designated general trading companies and a variety of export cartels. The state became the main actor and vehicle for pushing labor-intensive exports in the 1970s and more capital-intensive industries since the mid-1980s.[19]

The developmental state in Taiwan was characterized by the coherent leadership of the political elite. The Confucian ideal of rule by an educated elite gave way to rule by technocrats who were assumed to be knowledgeable about, and sympathetic toward, the interests of all segments of society. These technocrats, recruited by "technocrat patrons" within the state hierarchy, set national goals and priorities and mobilized resources and public attention for collective tasks. The state saw itself as the embodiment of the national destiny, and hence it had the obligation to tell everyone what needed to be done and censor divisive ideas and initiatives. This is one of the most important requirements of the success of state intervention in the market system and economic life.[20]

The strong state in Taiwan controlled foreign trade to raise revenue and expand technological and supply capacities. Therefore, the state apparatus in Taiwan departed significantly from the liberal and dependency perspectives of free trade. The regime contained a substantial amount of industry and trade bias. State-owned enterprises and cartels were established and the state manipulated the complex "import tariff-cum-export rebate" system to promote exports.[21] Aside from the existence of a tough growth-committed political leadership and a national consensus on goals, state activism in Taiwan was based on the state's real economic power, which derived from state ownership of banks or loanable funds rather than from mere political authority. The state's financial control over big business worked as a highly discretionary and qualitatively different control instrument that was not available in weak states. Public enterprises undertook initiatives which affected the whole configuration of the industry; the state made sizable resources available to private firms in return for their moving into state-specified directions.[22]

The East Asian developmental states have been involved in creating the conditions for economic growth and industrial adaptation, yet unlike the socialist states, they have refrained from exercising direct control. The "East Asian high-growth system" includes, first, stable rule by a political-bureaucratic elite not acceding to political demands that would undermine economic growth; second, cooperation between the public and private sectors under the overall guidance of a pilot planning agency; and third, a government that understands the need to use and respect methods of economic intervention based on the price mechanism.[23] The East Asian developmental states are also different from the "predatory states" in some African countries. In these countries, the state is the agency through which one class exploits the interests of other classes. The elite in predatory states extracts many resources from society but provides few "collective goods." This situation constitutes a barrier to economic transformation in the less-developed countries.[24]

The developmental state works with and often promotes the market. The market is employed as an instrument of development policies by exposing particular industries to international competitive pressures. A selective industrial policy for economic development that leads the market involves the following: (1) state initiatives as to what products or technologies should be encouraged; (2) public resources or influence over private resources to carry through these initiatives; and (3) a big before-the-fact plan or strategy.[25] Developmental states are characterized by tightly organized, relatively small-scale bureaucratic structures with the Weberian characteristics of highly selective, meritocratic recruitment patterns and long-term career rewards, which enhance the solidarity and the corporate identity of the bureaucratic elite.[26]

However, the strong-state paradigm also has its weaknesses. One salient characteristic of state capacity is its "unevenness" over time and in different policy spheres. The Japanese state may be autonomous in initiating industrial policies, but its agriculture and education policies have been highly constrained by the ruling Liberal Democratic Party and the corporatist interests of big business. Moreover, due to foreign pressure and its inability to use the Special Measure Law to enhance industrial cooperation, MITI has experienced a relative decline since the mid-1970s and has replaced direct intervention in industrial policies with "administrative guidance."[27] This creates a mixture of the "develop-mental state" and the "regulatory state" in Japan.

The strong-state paradigm also fails to analyze the political economy of the East Asian newly industrialized countries (NICs) in the era of democratic transition. In the case of Taiwan, democratization has led to a split in the state elite and created a new form of state-society interaction. The state elite is no longer a coherent body, nor can technocrats remain insulated from political interference. The rise of private firms and the decline of state-owned enterprises has weakened the capacity of the state to lead the market through interventionist policies. The state lacks clear national goals and priorities of development and has failed to mobilize resources and public attention for collective tasks with its legal forces. In brief, the emergence of a new type of state-society relationship since the late 1980s calls for the development of a new theoretical framework beyond the strong-state paradigm.

In conclusion, the East Asian NICs took advantage of their position as "late-comers" in a pro-trade international system in the 1950s and 1960s. However, we cannot attribute their economic success to autonomous bureaucratic capacities alone. We have to understand not only the state as an institution but also the politics of society as a whole: the interaction among the state apparatus, state-business relations, subcontract coordination, regionalism, and the like. This point is of special importance because as the state becomes more interest-represented and democratically accountable, we need to take a closer look at the process of state-society interaction if we are to understand policymaking in the transitional East Asian developmental states.

An Overview

The state-centered approach adopted in this study focuses on both the process and impact of Taiwan's cross-Straits economic policy. The study will discuss, first, the autonomy and capacities of the state as an actor in realizing the goals of its economic policy toward China and, second, the impact of the state-society relationship on the politics of this aspect of Taiwan's policymaking. The state-centered approach is not a state-only approach. In the discussion of cross-Straits economic relations, it facilitates the analysis of interaction between business interests and state initiatives and the capacity of the state to lead and reverse the market mechanism. The case of cross-Straits economic policymaking serves as an example to test the validity of the strong-state paradigm in the post-democratization era.

The focus of this book is the changing role of the Taiwanese state in policymaking during the period of political and economic transition. This study does not merely emphasize the institutional and legal perspectives of state actions. On the contrary, it concentrates on the change in the essential nature of the state, conflicts within the state, influences from social groups on state policies, interaction between state and society, and the effect of state actions on the market mechanism.

Chapter 2 discusses the process of democratization in Taiwan and its impact on cross-Straits relations. Chiang Ching-kuo's decision to open up the regime is identified as the event that crystallized the contradiction within Taiwanese society during the authoritarian years. Although there is no clear-cut "moment of democratization," the democratization process has acted as a catalyst for the split in the political elite and the convergence of technocrats and local interests, thus creating a dynamic civil society capable of resisting state intervention in both economic and political affairs. All these developments have affected the capacity of the state bureaucracy to initiate coherent policies. Hence, this chapter provides a general framework for a new type of state-society bargaining in cross-Straits policies.

Given the fact that both Taiwan and China are trying to manipulate cross-Straits economic interaction through political means, Chapter 3 will analyze the general trend of Taiwan's policy toward China and China's reunification policy. "Economic rationality" is distorted in this special kind of economic relationship, and this chapter will help to illuminate the "irrationality" and political momentum behind Taiwan's cross-Straits policy. It discusses the evolution of the People's Republic of China's (PRC's) national unification policy and then analyzes proposals for Taiwan independence raised by Taiwan's biggest opposition party. Particular attention will be paid to how the Taiwanese state responds to pressure from China and how the state accommodates the issue of national identity and unification by operating in the "gray area" between a one-China policy and Taiwan independence.

By the same token, the importance of politics in cross-Straits economic policy will be emphasized in the discussion of institutional conflicts within Taiwan's "mainland affairs" bureaucracies. Chapter 4 demonstrates that interagency conflicts result partly from the split in the political elite precipitated by the democratization process and partly from the political-economic tangles of cross-Straits policies. This discussion will show that Taiwan's bureaucratic elite is no longer a coherent body. Institutional conflicts also influence the capacity of the state to initiate timely and effective policies to regulate cross-Straits trade and investment.

Whereas the previous chapters describe the transformation of the Taiwanese state in the era of democracy, the last two chapters will evaluate the autonomy of the state and its capacity to lead the market mechanism in cross-Straits economic relations. In Chapter 5 it is argued that the ascendance of civil society, especially the business community, has led to a new type of state-society interaction. The role of big business groups in Taiwanese politics in general and in cross-Straits policy in particular will be analyzed. The major channels, means, and impact of business influence will be illustrated. Special emphasis will be put on the increasing importance of big-business interests in China and the corporatist style of bargaining between the state and the business community.

In Chapter 6, the other aspect of the new state-society relationship is considered; namely, the ability of the post-authoritarian state to control the market mechanism in cross-Straits trade and investment. It is argued that the state has failed to utilize macroeconomic policies and legal restrictions to regulate the profit-seeking activities of Taiwanese businesspeople. What really controls business is not the actions of the state but economic profit. In order to demonstrate the failure of the state's regulatory capacities, the author will use both official and private statistical data to recalculate trade and investment values. However, this chapter looks not only at Taiwan's dependence on the China market but also at China's growing dependence on Taiwan. This relationship of interdependence limits the state's power to reduce or moderate economic relations on both sides of the Taiwan Straits, and it is leading to the emergence of a "Greater China," which may have an immense impact on the international political economy.

In sum, the basic structure of political forces within Taiwan and Taiwan's pattern of external economic relations have been transformed in the 1990s, and the government's handling of cross-Straits trade and investment provides a good illustration of these transformations. By providing an economic opportunity that is irresistibly attractive to business interests while at the same time posing a political embarrassment to the state, cross-Straits trade and investment have served as a lever by which societal interests have moved an unwilling state. The analysis of cross-Straits economic policies reveals a sharp contrast between the state's role in governing the market in Taiwan's authoritarian past and its current role in the era of democratization. It underlines the three most crucial driving forces of Taiwan's political economy—democratization, state-society interaction, and economic interdependence with China—and provides insights into Taiwan's political and economic development in the 1990s and beyond.

Notes

1. For the purpose of simplicity, "China" refers to the People's Republic of China on the Chinese mainland; "Taiwan" refers to the Republic of China on the island of Taiwan.

2. Robert K. Yin, *Case Study Research* (Newbury Park, Calif.: Sage, 1989), 23.

3. Chien-kuo Pang, *The State and Economic Transformation: The Taiwan Case* (New York: Garland Publishing, 1992), 17.

4. For a more comprehensive introduction to these three schools, see John Ikenberry, David Lake, and Michael Mastanduno, *The State and American Foreign Economic Policy* (Ithaca: Cornell University Press, 1988).

5. Max Weber, *From Max Weber: Essays in Sociology,* trans. and ed. H. H. Gerth and C. Wright Mills (New York: Oxford University Press, 1958), 78.

6. For Weber's discussion on the state and bureaucracy, see Max Weber, "Types of Legitimate Domination," in vol. 1 of *Economy and Society* (New York: Bedminster Press, 1968), 212–301; Weber, "Bureaucracy," ibid., vol. 2, 956–1005.

7. Theda Skocpol, *States and Social Revolution* (Cambridge: Cambridge University Press, 1979), 29.

8. Alfred Stepan, *The State and Society: Peru in Comparative Perspective* (Princeton: Princeton University Press, 1978), xii. See also his discussion in *Rethinking Military Politics: Brazil and the Southern Cone* (Princeton: Princeton University Press, 1988), chapter 1.

9. Guillermo O'Donnell, "On the State, Democratization and Some Conceptual Problems: Latin American View with Glances at Some Post-Communist Countries," *World Development* 21, no. 8 (1993):1356; Guillermo O'Donnell, *Bureaucratic Authoritarianism: Argentina, 1966–1973, in Comparative Perspective* (Berkeley: University of California Press, 1988), chapter 1.

10. Gerald Rosenberg, *The Hollow Hope: Can Courts Bring About Social Change?* (Chicago: University of Chicago Press, 1991).

11. See Stephen Krasner, "Approaches to the State: Alternative Conceptions and Historical Dynamics," *Comparative Politics* 16, no. 2 (January 1984):223–246.

12. James Caporaso and David Levine, *Theories of Political Economy* (Cambridge: Cambridge University Press, 1992), 182–183.

13. Ikenberry, Lake, and Mastanduno, *The State and American Foreign Economic Policy*, 10–12; Peter Katzenstein, "Conclusion: Domestic Structures and Strategies of Foreign Economic Policy," in *Between Power and Plenty*, ed. Peter Katzenstein (Madison: University of Wisconsin Press, 1978), 295–337; Peter Katzenstein, ed., *Small States in World Markets* (Ithaca: Cornell University Press, 1986).

14. Stephen Krasner, "Policy Making in a Weak State," in *American Foreign Policy: Theoretical Essays,* ed. John Ikenberry (Boston: Scott, Foresman, and Company, 1989), 293–295; see also Stephen Krasner, *Defending the National Interest* (Princeton: Princeton University Press, 1987), 55–90.

15. For discussion of the concept of developmental states, see Chalmers Johnson, *MITI and the Japanese Miracle* (Stanford: Stanford University Press, 1982); Steve Chan, *East Asian Dynamism* (Boulder: Westview Press, 1990); Richard Samuels, *The Business of the Japanese State* (Ithaca: Cornell University Press, 1988).

16. Johnson, *MITI and the Japanese Miracle*, chapter 6.

17. Pang, *The State and Economic Transformation*, chapter 2 and chapter 8; Thomas Gold, "Entrepreneurs, Multinationals, and the State," in *Contending Approaches to the Political Economy of Taiwan*, ed. Edwin Winckler and Susan Greenhalgh (New York: M. E. Sharpe, 1988), 175–206.

18. Stephan Haggard, *Pathways from the Periphery* (Ithaca: Cornell University Press, 1990), chapter 3; Fred Deyo, *Beneath the Miracle: Labor Subordination in the New Asian Industrialism* (Berkeley: University of California Press, 1989).

19. Alice Amsden, *Asia's Next Giant: South Korea and Late Industrialization* (Oxford: Oxford University Press, 1989).

20. For a cultural explanation of the strong developmental state, see Lucian Pye, "The New Asian Capitalism: A Political Portrait," in *In Search of an East Asian Development Model*, ed. Peter Berger and Hsin-huang Hsiao (New Brunswick, New Jersey: Transaction Books, 1988), 81–99; Tu Wei-ming ed., *The Confucian World*

Observed: A Contemporary Discussion of Confucian Humanism in East Asia (Honolulu, Hawaii: Institute of Culture and Communication, The East-West Center, 1992); for the role of technocrats in Taiwan's development, see Li Cheng and Lynn White, "Elite Transformation and Modern Change in Mainland China and Taiwan: Empirical Data and the Theory of Technocracy," *China Quarterly*, no. 121 (March 1990):1–35.

21. Robert Wade, *Governing the Market* (Princeton: Princeton University Press, 1990). See also Stephan Haggard, *Pacific Dynamics: The International Politics of Industrial Change* (Boulder: Westview Press, 1989).

22. Robert Wade, "Industrial Policy in East Asia: Does It Lead or Follow the Market?" in *Manufacturing Miracles*, ed. Gary Gereffi and Donald Wyman (Princeton: Princeton University Press, 1990), 247. See also Kuen Lee, *New East Asian Economic Development* (New York: M. E. Sharpe, 1993).

23. Chalmers Johnson, "Political Institutions and Economic Performance: The Government-Business Relationship in Japan, South Korea, and Taiwan," in *Asian Economic Development: Present and Future*, ed. Robert Scalapino, Seizaburo Sato, and Jusfu Wanandi (Berkeley: Institute of Asian Studies, University of California, 1985), 71.

24. Robert Fatton, *Predatory Rule: State and Civil Society in Africa* (Boulder: Lynne Rienner, 1992).

25. See Wade, "Industrial Policy in East Asia," 234.

26. Ziya Onis, "The Logic of the Developmental State," *Comparative Politics* 24, no. 1 (October 1991):124.

27. David Friedman, *The Misunderstood Miracle* (Ithaca: Cornell University Press, 1988).

2

Democratic Transition in Taiwan

The most salient change in Taiwan since 1988 has been the transition from an authoritarian to a democratic regime. During the authoritarian era, state policies were initiated by autonomous technocrats and the supreme leaders, Chiang Kai-shek and his son Chiang Ching-kuo. Political participation was limited to the local level, and civil society rarely made itself heard in the policymaking process at the national level.

Democratization has released social forces in Taiwan. As demands for democracy increased within civil society, the biggest opposition party alternately prodded the state and cooperated with it in opening the regime to free competition. The ascendance of social forces and the split in the state itself have led to a change in the rules of the political game and introduced new actors into the policymaking process.

The ultimate goal of this book is to understand the change in state-society relations and its impact on policymaking in Taiwan. This chapter will focus on the most important factor in the shift of the balance of power between the state and society—democratic transition. Discussion of the democratization process will help us understand differences within the state elite regarding the speed and content of democratization, what major actors have emerged in the process of democratization, and how the reformers in the state have allied with moderate factions in society to achieve a political breakthrough. Conflict and cooperation among these new actors have created a new type of state-society interaction in Taiwan. This new type of interaction will have a profound influence on state capacities and state autonomy in initiating market-conforming policies.

This chapter will first analyze two theories of democratization—the structural and the process approaches to democratic transition. In Taiwan's case, the formation of alliances between the state and society and elite ambition within the state can be best explained by the process-oriented approach to democratization. To grasp the essence of state-society interaction, this chapter will not emphasize the reasons for democratization. Instead, it will focus on the early stage of top-down liberalization in Taiwan, the division within the state and society, the emergence of a state-society alliance, and the consolidation of the reformers in Taiwan.

Theories of Democratic Transition

Whereas structure-oriented scholars of comparative politics and social change focus on the "driving forces" behind or the "preconditions" for democracy, process-oriented theorists are more interested in the strategic calculations of the actors in democratic transition.[1] These two approaches are not mutually exclusive but complementary.

The Structural Perspective

Theorists of democratic transition point to various structural factors leading to democratization, including religious changes, new policies of external actors, and the demonstration or "snowball effect" of democratic transition.[2] Among these structural factors, economic development and the development of capitalism are the driving forces of democratization. They introduce the market system and thus create or revive civil society. The rise of civil society and a strong middle class are two pillars of a stable democratic regime.

From the experience of Western democracies, it is clear that a peaceful democratic process is possible only when potentially disruptive strains are kept out of politics and settled in the market. Through the separation of politics and the economy, economic activities are conducted according to the laws of supply and demand instead of through authoritarian allocations by the state. The state's capacity to penetrate into the economic sphere is thus weakened. Under the free market system, the market mechanism provides consumer free choice, occupational free choice, and a wide range of other free choices. Without these, further political liberties are impossible.[3]

Hence, a free market system creates some preconditions of democracy. Robert Dahl argues that the emergence of a "Modern Dynamic Pluralist (MDP)" society is the precondition for the rise of a polyarchy.[4] An MDP society disperses power, influence, authority, and control away from any single center toward a variety of individuals, groups, associations, and organizations. Therefore, economic development diverts the economic power of the state and transfers it to consumers. Economic development and the market system not only separate economic and political power but also provide a check on state power.

Economic development also changes the class structure of society. For Barrington Moore, different types of class domination create different regime types. If the landed aristocracy is able to contain and dominate the commercial class, the authoritarian or fascist version of industrial modernization will occur, as was the case in pre–World War II Japan and Germany; if the commercial bourgeoisie, landlord class, and bureaucrats are too weak, intellectuals are politicized, and peasants take the lead, the result will be a communist revolution like that in Russia and China; if the commercialization of agriculture leads to the creation of a bourgeoisie and the subordination of the agricultural sector, democracy might emerge, as was the case in the United States and Great Britain.[5] Capitalist development will tip the balance of power in favor of the middle and working classes, and the subordinate class will fight for democracy while the ruling class will support the status quo.[6]

Economic development and the development of a market economy create civil society. Civil society, conceived as an aggregate of institutions whose members are engaged primarily in a complex of non-state activities, exercises all sorts of pressures or controls on state institutions.[7] Any fundamental political transformation of the capitalist system requires a rejection of state authority by civil society. Furthermore, Linz indicates that the emergence of "autonomous intermediate groups" based on class, occupation, region, ethnicity, or religion can provide the basis for the limitation of state power and for democratic political institutions as the most effective means by which society can exercise control over the state.[8]

From the structural perspective, economic development and the market economy enable the bourgeoisie to limit state power and exploit democratic means to serve its own interests. The state has to negotiate with influential social groups and the middle class during the process of policymaking and policy implementation. These bargaining and negotiation processes between the state and society provide crucial democratic impulses that emphasize compromise and a non-zero-sum game of democratic rules. Furthermore, contacts with the world market and liberal democratic culture give the market-oriented nations more opportunities to learn about and shape the democratic political culture, which is crucial to the emergence and consolidation of democratic values.

To sum up, economic development not only changes the material base of authoritarian regimes, it also creates a "private" sphere independent from state control. Civil society is not merely "independent" of state control; it requires more resources and privileges and the reallocation of political values. Hence, civil society is no longer satisfied with "top-down" liberalization bestowed by the state. It will struggle to protect its wealth through political means, thus promoting interaction between state and society and beginning the process of democratization.

The Process Perspective

In contrast to the macro perspective on democratization provided by the structural approach, the process perspective regards economic development and cultural heritage as conditioned factors promoting or impeding democratization. Structural factors can explain why democratization happens but fail to explain what the outcome of democratization will be. Hence, a process-oriented study of democratization focuses on political actors and their interaction and on the way this leads to different types of democratic transition.

The process-oriented approach emphasizes divisions in the state and differentiation in society. Democratization is an action of both state and society. O'Donnell and Schmitter have identified four different political actors in the process of democratization: hard-liners and reformers inside the authoritarian state, and moderates and radicals in the opposition bloc.[9] Based on this distinction, Przeworski argues that liberalization is a result of interaction between divisions in the authoritarian regime and the autonomous organization of civil society. Popular mobilization signals to the potential liberalizers the possibility of an alliance that could change the relations of forces within the power bloc to their advantage; visible splits in the power bloc indicate to civil society that political space may have been opened for autonomous organization. Hence, popular mobilization and divisions in the regime feed on each other.[10]

Samuel Huntington also subscribes to the interactive perspective of democratization. He identifies three different types of democratic transition: (1) *transformation:* top-down democratization in which those in power in the authoritarian regime take the lead and play the decisive role in ending that regime and changing it into a democratic system; (2) *replacement:* a bottom-up form of democratization that results from the opposition gaining strength in relation to the government until the latter collapses or is overthrown; and (3) *transplacement:* whereby democratization is produced by the combined actions of government and opposition. In the third type of democratization, the balance between standpatters and reformers within the government is such that the government is willing to negotiate a change of regime but is unwilling to initiate it. It has to be pushed and pulled into formal or informal negotiations with the opposition. Within the opposition, democratic moderates are strong enough to prevail over antidemocratic radicals, but they are not strong enough to overthrow the government. Therefore, they too see virtues in negotiation.[11]

The most important concern of democratic transition is how to create a "consolidated" and "stable" democracy. One salient distinction between liberalization and democratization is that the latter is an "institutionalized" liberalization. The regime must first expand political participation and then channel and moderate rising demands for further participation. For Huntington, the principal agent of institutionalization is political parties.[12] Stepan goes further to argue that between the state and civil society, there exists a "political society" that includes political parties, elections, electoral rules, and legislatures. A full democratic transition must involve political society, and the composition and consolidation of a democratic polity must entail serious thought and action about the core institutions of a democratic political society.[13]

One crucial element of the process-oriented approach to democratization is the importance it gives to the rule making and institutionalization process between the state and society. The goal of democratization is to create a situation of coexistence between the two. In this situation, none of the players would lose completely in all arenas. Coexistence depends on establishing rules for the democratic game that provide institutionalized channels of compromise and coexistence and an atmosphere of mutual trust and tolerance. The essence of transition is to outline in advance the rules of the game—the norms, procedures, and institutions whose operation should allow a fair balance of winning and losing. Using Di Palma's words, the outcome of democratization is uncertain, but the rule of democratization cannot be uncertain.[14]

To sum up, the process-oriented approach focuses on strategic calculations, processes, and sequential patterns that are involved in moving from one type of political regime to another, especially under conditions of nonviolence, gradualism, and social continuity. Structural factors such as history, political culture, and economic development limit the alternatives available to participants, but the process of democratization is determined by interaction between the state and society. The combined actions of the state and society establish a new set of rules for the democratic game. Interaction among different factions within the state and society creates different types of democratic transition.

Democratic Transition in Taiwan

Taiwan's democratization has been conducted through the combined forces of state and society. Economic development created an influential and prosperous middle class that demanded more political rights. The state gradually opened up the regime and established channels of communication with social forces. After the death of the authoritarian leader, the state began to split into competing factions. Reformers allied with moderate factions in civil society to attack the conservative camp within the state. Power struggles and alliances involved the issue of constitutional revision, that is, the making of the rules of the democratic game. In the following pages, the first subject of analysis will be the top-down liberalization initiated by President Chiang Ching-kuo; this will be followed by discussion of the split in the state and state-society interaction. Finally, the focus will shift to the consolidation of the reformers' power in Taiwan.

Initiation of Democratization

Taiwan's democratization under Chiang Ching-kuo was a top-down transition or "transformation" type of political change, according to Samuel Huntington's classification. Using his immense power within the state hierarchy, Chiang subdued the conservative force in the state, opened a dialogue with opposition groups, and skillfully led social forces into the institutionalized framework of state-society interaction.

The year 1986 was a turning point in Taiwanese politics. Knowing that his health was poor and being aware that the regime was under rising social pressure, Chiang decided to launch a large-scale political reform. In early 1986 he declared that no member of his own family would succeed him as president of the Republic of China (ROC). In March, Chiang appointed a twelve-member ad hoc committee of ranking officials to study the subject of political reform. They recommended a program of reform measures including the termination of martial law, the lifting of the ban on rival political parties, and the reorganization of the parliament to allow a strong representation by native Taiwanese. Chiang also approved a "dialogue" between officials of the ruling Kuomintang and leaders of opposition groups.[15]

In September that year, Taiwan's biggest opposition group, known as the *dangwai* (literally "outside the party"), jumped the gun and formed Taiwan's first opposition party, the Democratic Progressive Party (DPP). Instead of ordering the Taiwan Garrison Command to suppress the new party, Chiang resisted pressure from the military and security sectors and took no action to arrest opposition leaders. Chiang declared the DPP illegal but signaled to society that martial law and the ban on political parties would soon be lifted. In the supplementary elections to the Legislative Yuan held shortly after the DPP's formation, the new party captured 24.6 percent of the popular vote and fourteen seats.[16]

Before Chiang finally lifted martial law and began the process of liberalization in 1987, his major goal was to incorporate opposition forces into the institutional framework. Chiang adopted a policy of selective coercion to suppress rather than eliminate opposition forces, thus allowing them to go around the edges of legal limits. He also established formal channels of communication with the *dangwai*. Chiang's skillful political maneuvering to some degree undermined the radical forces in the opposition group and encouraged the moderate factions to play the game.

The events of 1987 were in large part initiated from the top down, but opposition forces in society played an important role in pushing the state toward reform. Chiang's tactful policy of selective suppression meant that the opposition force he faced was at the same time one that was exerting enormous pressure on him, and one that he could talk to.[17] Robust economic performance and long years of political stability had given the KMT party-state enough momentum to control the reform agenda, but liberalization would never have been implemented had the opposition remained weak. State coherence was maintained by the unchallenged power of the supreme leader, and there was no informal alliance between the state and society. But communication channels had already been established. The split in the state and closer state-society interaction did not appear until after the death of Chiang Ching-kuo in early 1988.

State Coherence in the Early Stage of Democratization

In the early stage of Taiwan's democratization, the political elite, most members of which were Chiang's clients, united to resist ultraconservative forces within the state hierarchy. There existed a rough balance of power among the political elite, and they had common enemies to fight.

Chiang died on January 13, 1988, and he was succeeded by his vice president, Lee Teng-hui, the following day. Between January 13 and January 27, when a special meeting of the KMT Central Standing Committee was held and an acting party chairman was elected, there was a power vacuum in the KMT party-state. Backed by the secretary-general of the KMT, Lee Huan, and the chief of the general staff, Hau Pei-tsun, public opinion and the party elite were mobilized to support Chiang's legal successor Lee Teng-hui as acting chairman of the ruling party. During this period, a strategic alliance among the two Lees and Hau emerged when James Soong, the party's deputy secretary-general, launched a surprise attack on ultraconservatives who proposed that the Central Standing Committee meeting should be postponed until July.[18] Lee was elected acting chairman on January 27, 1988.

From January 27 to July 7, 1988, when the KMT's Thirteenth Party Congress was convened, political forces within the KMT reached a balance of power. Whereas Lee Teng-hui was the president and acting chairman of the party, Lee Huan controlled the party apparatus and General Hau Pei-tsun ruled the military. At the congress, Lee Huan topped the ballot for the Central Committee and Hau's tenure as chief of general staff was renewed for an eighth term. As for Lee Teng-hui, he was left as *primus inter pares*, lacking a substantial power base. In June 1989 Lee Huan became premier, and a triple alliance consisting of the two Lees and Hau was established.

During the two years 1988–1990, the KMT party-state went through a process of power reconstruction. The state invoked "backward legitimacy" and stressed elements of continuity with the past. Lee was a symbol of the continuity of Chiang Ching-kuo's reforms, but his power was constrained by Chiang's political clients from the authoritarian era both in the party and the military system. During this period, few substantial political reform policies were launched.

The Split in the State

The year 1990 was a watershed in Taiwan's democratization. After two years of peaceful transformation, the KMT party-state finally split into two groups, a National Affairs Conference was convened, and the process of constitutional amendment began.

The main task of the meeting of the KMT Central Committee in February 1990 was to select presidential and vice presidential candidates. During the process of selecting a vice presidential candidate, Lee Teng-hui was challenged by Lee Huan, Lin Yang-kang, and their followers, who proposed that the committee democratically elect a candidate. The meeting ultimately rejected this proposal and confirmed Lee's appointment of Li Yuan-zu as his running mate. In late February, the anti–Lee Teng-hui alliance nominated Lin Yang-kang and Chiang Ching-kuo's half brother Wego Chiang as presidential and vice presidential candidates. Thus two opposing groups were formed within the KMT—the "mainstream alliance" that supported Lee Teng-hui and the "nonmainstream alliance" that supported Lee Huan, Hau Pei-tsun, and others.[19]

The nonmainstream alliance collapsed at the last minute partly because the president and his supporters made it clear that a challenge to Lee Teng-hui amounted to a coup against the native Taiwanese. This "conspiracy theory" was popularized by mainstream legislators.[20] This was the first occasion on which Lee mobilized public opinion and social sentiment in support of a Taiwanese president and to suppress his opponents within the state. Lee was elected president by the National Assembly in March 1990. In May, to everyone's surprise, Lee appointed Hau Pei-tsun as premier in place of Lee Huan.

The appointment of Hau did not represent a retreat on Lee Teng-hui's part. On the contrary, Lee was playing the trick of "divide and rule" to split the nonmainstream group. After Lee Huan's triumph at the Thirteenth Party Congress, the only way Lee Teng-hui could offset the ambitious premier was to unite with another pillar of the triple alliance—Hau Pei-tsun. This not only split the nonmainstream group but also exposed Hau, an authoritarian military figure, to attacks from the opposition and the general public. The same day Lee nominated Hau as premier, a mass movement was organized by the DPP to oppose Hau. What is more important, to become premier, Hau had to abandon the barracks and return to civilian life. This gave Lee an opportunity to penetrate the military, especially its personnel affairs, and to command the military in his capacity as head of state. All in all, Lee skillfully manipulated conflicts within the nonmainstream group, exposed mainlander politicians to public attack, utilized his popularity and his status as a native Taiwanese president to mobilize support within society, and then strengthened his power base by penetrating the military. After gradually consolidating his power, Lee then introduced bolder democratic reform policies.

Factionalism Within the Opposition Camp

The forces of political opposition within civil society play the role of forcing the state to reform. As Antonio Gramsci has argued, any fundamental political transformation of a capitalist system requires a rejection of the state authority by the civil society, which includes all those organizations commonly thought of as "private."[21] However, in Taiwan's case, most "autonomous" social movements organized since the lifting of martial law have been politicized and mobilized by the opposition party. Hence, civil society alone cannot force the state to reform. It is the political party that channels social discontent and serves as an agent for civil society. The DPP has acted as a competing force with the KMT, voicing dissident opinions in society.

However, during the process of democratization, a radical opposition force can encourage the survival or revival of repressive forces in the state that would lead to an overall crackdown. A radical opposition may also mobilize a mass movement and result in a bottom-up revolution. Only when moderate factions control the radical forces within the opposition camp can political dialogue between the state and civil society be opened and channels of communication established.

Factionalism is not new within the DPP camp. The two major factions are the New Tide and Formosa, the Middle faction adopts a neutral stance between the two, and the Independence Alliance is a relatively new faction advocating a radical independence policy.[22] Disputes between the two big factions have mainly centered on two themes: (1) whether the DPP should take an explicit stand in favor of Taiwan independence, and (2) which strategy the party should employ, parliamentary struggle or mass movement. In the early days of the party, New Tide, composed mainly of young intellectuals (some of them working for various anti-KMT magazines), took the position that the DPP should immediately announce its support for Taiwan independence and should work more actively for that cause. They also maintained that the party should use mass protest movements as its main strategy.[23]

Formosa, composed mainly of party officeholders or former officeholders, has advocated that the DPP should concentrate for the time being on the issue of constitutional reform. Although Formosa members do not overlook the importance of mass movements, they believe that the party's main strategy should be one of electoral-parliamentary struggle. They have argued that the main task of the DPP is to form alliances with social movements instead of becoming a "class party" and politicizing social movements. The strategy they have advocated is one of "besieging the center from the periphery," which involves contesting local elections, especially for county magistrates, and pressing the KMT to reform.[24]

The radical New Tide faction dominated the policymaking center when the DPP was established in 1986. After the lifting of martial law and the release of opposition leaders Huang Hsin-chieh and Chang Chun-hung, Formosa began to incorporate minor factions such as the Forward faction and the Middle faction and as a result gradually captured power within the DPP. At the DPP's Third Congress the Formosa leader Huang Hsin-chieh was elected party chairman and his faction became the majority. From 1988 to 1991, Formosa was the real power within the DPP. New Tide experienced a revival at the Fifth Congress in 1991 after allying with dissidents returned from abroad, but Formosa member Hsu Hsin-liang was elected as chairman. The two main factions reached a rough balance of power at that time, with Formosa enjoying a small majority. Figure 2.1 illustrates the faction and power structure of the DPP.

A successful transition to democracy requires that a moderate faction control radical forces within the opposition camp and reach agreement with reformers within the state. The most important factor contributing to the success of moderate forces in the DPP is electoral competition. From 1989 to 1994, Taiwan held major elections almost every year. The DPP's poor performance in the 1991 National Assembly election taught it a lesson that radical appeals for Taiwan independence and bottom-up revolution could not win votes. Since 1991, the DPP has wisely shifted its focus from mass movements to public policy issues. The party did formally adopt a proindependence platform, but this stance has been moderated to attract voters whose political attitudes are in the gray area between unification and independence.

During the 1992 Legislative Yuan election, all the major factions joined the campaign and the DPP captured fifty seats, one third of the total. Leaders of the New Tide and Independence Alliance factions entered the Legislative Yuan and adopted the same "parliamentary line" as the moderates in the party. Elections encourage the DPP to play the game and

FIGURE 2.1   Factional Politics and Factional Seats in DPP Central
Standing Committee, 1986–1991

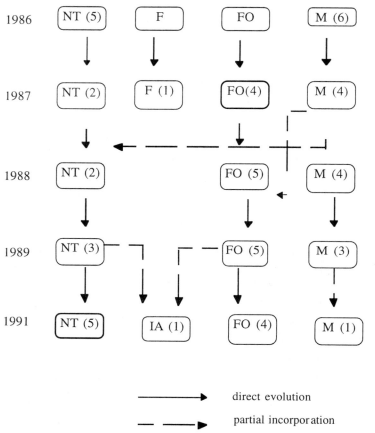

direct evolution

partial incorporation

Numbers within the parentheses indicate seats in the Central Standing Committee

NT: New Tide Faction   F: Forward Faction   FO: Formosa Faction
M: Middle Faction   IA: Independence Alliance Faction

At the Sixth Congress of the DPP in 1994, the Middle Faction divided into two loose
groups—the "Justice Alliance" and the "Welfare State Alliance."

SOURCE: Huang, Teh-fu, *Minzhu jingbudang yu Taiwan diqu zhengzhi minzhuhua* (The
Democratic Progressive Party and Taiwan's Democratization) (Taipei: Shih-ying, 1992)
81, 85.

moderate its radical policies in order to win votes. Furthermore, as the DPP captures a bigger share of the popular vote (see Figure 2.2), the parliamentary party caucus will play the dominant role in the DPP's policy-making. Reliance on mass movements may diminish, and ultraradical factions will be weakened. The DPP will become an institutionalized opposition party willing to follow the democratic rules of the game.

The Emergence of State-Society Alliances

The liberalization policies initiated by Chiang Ching-kuo were the first step toward democratization. However, throughout the Chiang era, the authoritarian constitutional setup remained intact. Between his assumption of the KMT chairmanship in 1988 and his inauguration as president in 1990, Lee Teng-hui gradually built up his personal reputation and enhanced his power base. Constitutional reform was finally launched in 1990.

As Adam Przeworski argues, outcomes of democratic transition are uncertain and indeterminate *ex ante*. It is the "people" and political forces competing to promote their interests and value who determine what these outcomes will be.[25] Lee Teng-hui skillfully maneuvered forces outside the state to gain political ground within the regime and used a strategic alliance with the opposition party and mass movements to attack conservative forces and promote democratization.

In mid-1990, the upper house of parliament, the National Assembly, consisting mainly of deputies elected in China shortly before the Nationalist government transferred to Taiwan, was convened to elect a new president of the ROC. Senior members of the National Assembly took the opportunity to demand a salary increase and an expansion of their privileges. This behavior, added to general discontent with the power struggle within the KMT, provoked a Tiananmen Square–style student demonstration at the Chiang Kai-shek Memorial Hall in downtown Taipei in March. Strengthened in their position by massive media coverage and public sympathy, the students called for the abolition of the National Assembly, the long overdue termination of the "Temporary Provisions" of the constitution, the holding of a national constitutional convention to resolve the constitutional and political crisis, and the formulation of a timetable for reform.[26]

The student movement provided the necessary catalyst for Lee's reforms. The president promised to convene a National Affairs Conference and set a timetable for constitutional reform. The day after these concessions were announced, students retreated from the Memorial Hall and the movement came to a peaceful end.[27] This incident demonstrated how Lee Teng-hui not only managed to coexist with social forces

FIGURE 2.2 The Percentage of Popular Vote of KMT and DPP

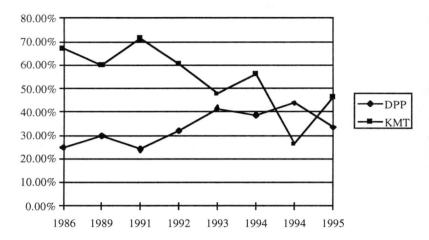

Year		DPP	KMT
1986	Supplementary Election of Legislative Yuan and National Assembly	24.60%	66.70%
1989	County Magistrate and Legislative Yuan Election	29.70%	59.70%
1991	National Assembly Election	23.94%	71.17%
1992	Legislative Yuan Election	31.86%	60.50%
1993	County Magistrate Election	41.30%	47.47%
1994	Taiwan Governor Election	38.72%	56.22%
1994	Taipei Mayor Election	43.68%	25.90%
1995	Legislative Yuan Election	33.17%	46.06%

SOURCE: I-Chou Liu, "Where Have All the Independent Voters Gone?" (paper presented at annual meeting of American Political Science Association, Washington, D.C., September 2–5, 1993); *Zhongyang ribao* (Central Daily News), December 4, 1994; *Zhongyang ribao,* December 3, 1995.

but also used them as a power base in his battle with the conservatives. In his inaugural address in May 1990, Lee finally announced that the "period of mobilization for the suppression of Communist rebellion" would shortly be terminated and that the parliaments would be reformed.[28] Interpretation No. 261, issued by the Council of Grand Justices on June 21, 1990, stated that all members of parliament frozen in office since their election on the mainland should resign by December 31, 1991.[29]

Lee's next step was to convince the DPP to attend the National Affairs Conference in order to "endorse" his constitutional reform. To everybody's surprise, Lee received DPP chairman Huang Hsin-chieh (a member of the Formosa faction) in the Presidential Office. After this meeting, Huang began to persuade his members to participate in the National Affairs Conference.[30] The conference achieved a consensus on three points: the need for a law to regulate relations between Taiwan and China, the direct election of the Taiwan governor, and parliamentary reform.[31]

During the National Affairs Conference, the most serious divergence between the KMT and the DPP occurred over the method of selecting the president. The DPP raised the "direct election" issue in opposition to the KMT's proposal for indirect elections through an electoral college. The DPP organized an opposition alliance at the conference and submitted "three principles" as the basis for negotiations: direct election of the president, a single-chamber parliament, and elections for the governor of Taiwan and the mayors of Taipei and Kaohsiung before 1992. The DPP even threatened to withdraw from the conference if its first request—direct presidential elections—was turned down. Before the July 2 deadline, James Soong, the secretary-general of the KMT, delivered a message from Lee Teng-hui agreeing to direct elections.[32] The DPP withdrew its boycott and the National Affairs Conference ended with a compromise between the two parties.

Lee and the moderate forces within the opposition needed each other at the National Affairs Conference. The opposition promised to participate in the conference but continued to press the state for more liberal reforms. Lee resisted conservative pressure, rescued the conference from collapse, and compromised with the DPP on the crucial issue of direct election of the president. Direct election became the focus of a further split within the state. It also served as a link between reformers within the state and moderates in society at large. The state-society alliance on this issue forced the conservative faction to retreat from the political scene.

Rulemaking and the Consolidation of the Reformers' Power

The conclusion of the National Affairs Conference marked the beginning of a new era in state-society interaction. The consensus reached at the conference was an agreement between reformers in the state and moderates in society. The constitutional amendment and electoral competition provided an institutionalized arena in which various social forces had significant political presence in the democratic system.

Constitutional revision in Taiwan has been characterized by gradualism. The KMT, although determined to manipulate the process, was willing to leave some room for negotiation. The first stage of constitutional revision, conducted by the unreformed National Assembly, took place in April 1991. By summoning an extraordinary session of the First National Assembly before its senior members were forcibly retired, the KMT ensured the passage of provisions relating to parliamentary elections and provided procedural legitimacy of the second National Assembly. The new National Assembly would then engage in more substantial constitutional revisions.[33]

Meanwhile, the DPP mobilized a mass movement to protest the revision of the constitution by senior members of the National Assembly and threatened to withdraw its members from the body. The KMT reached a hasty agreement with the DPP under which the latter's continued attendance at the National Assembly sessions was exchanged for revision of the president's emergency powers. As part of the compromise, the constitution was to allow for the establishment of the National Security Council, but it was agreed that regulations to legalize that body must be enacted before 1993. The DPP ended its demonstration; ten amendments to the constitution were passed, the "period of mobilization" was ended, and the accompanying Temporary Provisions of the constitution were abolished.[34]

Elections for the Second National Assembly were held in December 1991, and an extraordinary session of this body was convened in March 1992. The thorniest issues in the second stage constitutional revision were the powers of the president and whether to elect the president by direct popular ballot or by proxy vote in the National Assembly. Lee Teng-hui's pro-direct-election proposal was backed by public opinion and rising local demands. However, under great pressure from nonmainstream politicians, the special meeting of the KMT Central Standing Committee could reach no conclusion on this issue. Although there was a small majority favoring direct presidential elections, Lee decided to postpone the final decision, leaving it to the KMT's Central Committee.[35] Opposition to direct elections was so intense that the KMT decided to avoid the issue and not make any substantial amendments to the clause on presidential elections during the second stage of constitutional revision. Hence, the final text of Article 12 of the amendments states that "both the President and the Vice President shall be elected by the entire electorate in the free area of the ROC; the method of election shall be

decided by an extraordinary session of the National Assembly to be convened by the President before May 20, 1995."[36]

The extraordinary session of the Second National Assembly passed
eight additional articles to the constitution. In addition to having the
power to nominate the chairman and members of the Examination Yuan,
the chairman of the Judicial Yuan, and the members of the Council of
Grand Justices, the president, under additional Article 15, was empow-
ered to nominate the members of the Control Yuan. The Control Yuan also
lost the right to endorse the president's nominees for membership of the
Judicial and Examination Yuans, which was transferred to the National
Assembly.[37] The National Assembly was to hold regular sessions, during
which the president would deliver written and oral reports on the state of
the nation.[38]

On the most controversial issue of direct presidential elections, Lee
decided to compromise to buy time. He understood that public opinion
was on his side, and the opposition camp shared the same view. Lee's
strategy was to enhance the legal power of the presidency and then to
mobilize social forces to oust the antidemocratic forces.

After the collapse of Lee Huan's power, the only nonmainstream leader
who could challenge Lee Teng-hui was Premier Hau Pei-tsun. After a
short period of cooperation, conflicts began to emerge between Lee Teng-
hui and Hau. They differed on issues such as the premier's endorsement
power, policies toward national unification/independence, and the
power of the president. At the same time, Hau continued to intervene
directly in military affairs and officer appointments, which should have
been the prerogative of the president.

Therefore, Lee and the DPP had a common enemy to fight. Before the
1992 Legislative Yuan election, the DPP launched a campaign to attack the
then finance minister, Wang Chien-shien, on the issue of the land tax. The
DPP argued that by levying an extra land tax, the "mainlander minister"
was actually trying to deprive the Taiwanese of their property. The ultimate target was Wang's patron Premier Hau, also a mainlander. Wang
failed to get support from Lee and resigned under pressure from both the
KMT and the DPP. The downfall of Wang implied the further weakening
of Hau's nonmainstream power.

The main platform of the DPP's campaign during the Legislative Yuan
election at the end of 1992 was opposition to Hau Pei-tsun. The pressure
created by the DPP's performance in the election forced Hau to resign
finally in February 1993. He was replaced by Lee's client, Lien Chan.[39]

The KMT's Fourteenth Congress in August 1993 signaled the final consolidation of Lee's power. In order to pass reform measures and alter the
party's power structure, Lee decided to add 520 elected officials and
provincial, county, and city branch leaders to the slate of delegates,

enlarging the total number to 2,100 from 1,059 at the Thirteenth Congress. The addition of these extra delegates representing the party's grass roots ensured that <u>Lee's mainstream faction wo</u>uld be in the majority at the congress.[40] As a result of this maneuver, the nonmainstream faction won only 17 percent of the Central Committee seats, in contrast to the Thirteenth Congress in 1989, when they won a majority.[41]

After the Fourteenth Congress and the collapse of Hau's power, anti-Lee forces within the KMT hierarchy were marginalized. Soon after, a group of young nonmainstream legislators left the KMT and established the New Party. The 1994 round of constitutional revisions included provisions for direct election of the president and a reduction of the endorsement power of the premier. Hau Pei-tsun and Lin Yang-kang became increasingly alienated from Lee and the mainstream faction. This culminated in Lin's decision to stand for the presidency in the first direct election in March 1996. Hau Pei-tsun eventually agreed to be his running mate. During the 1995 Legislative Yuan election, Hau and Lin openly campaigned on behalf of New Party candidates, and in December 1995 they were finally expelled from the KMT.

Implications of Taiwan's Democratization

The outcome of democratization depends on the actions of participants, but no single force controls what occurs. The probability of a particular outcome is determined jointly by the institutional framework and the resources that the different political forces bring to the competition. In Taiwan, reformers led by Lee Teng-hui were fighting a two-front battle against both conservatives within the state and opposition forces in society. To win this battle, the reformers had to be adept at both manipulating and controlling social forces and had to set up priorities and make choices.

Lee's choice was to ally himself with moderate factions in society in order to control conservative forces within the state. Lee's priority was to divide the conservative forces and then to use the appeal of democratic reforms, such as direct presidential elections and the nationalization of the military, to form a strategic alliance with the opposition party and civil society. At the same time, by opening up electoral competition, Lee not only encouraged the moderation of radical forces in the opposition camp and their incorporation into the institutionalized democratic process but also mobilized public opinion as a power base for his struggle with nonmainstream politicians. As winning elections gradually became the first priority for the KMT, Lee promoted the "Taiwanization" of the party and recruited more native Taiwanese politicians into the state hierarchy. This policy signaled to society that the KMT party-state under Lee's leadership was to be an indigenous regime. However, it also intensified the subethnic conflict between "native Taiwanese" and "mainlanders."

This intensification of subethnic conflict was an unexpected outcome of democratization. As the preceding analysis illustrates, Taiwan's democratization was not a bottom-up revolution but a combined effort of state and society. One clear linkage between the reformist group in the state and the moderate group in society is that they are both composed of native Taiwanese.

Strictly speaking, the distinction between "Taiwanese" and mainlanders in Taiwan is minimal. Both groups came from the mainland originally; it is just that whereas the mainlanders followed Chiang Kai-shek's troops to Taiwan in 1949, native Taiwanese had begun to emigrate to Taiwan as early as three hundred years ago. They share the same ethnicity and customs, and intermarriage between mainlanders and Taiwanese is quite common. Subethnic conflicts originate from the tragic experience of the February 28 Incident and the "White Terror" of the early years of KMT rule in Taiwan. However, conflict was intensified during the process of democratization.

As Paul Brass argues, ethnicity is not "given" but is a social and political construction. It is the creation of the elite, who draw upon, distort, and sometimes fabricate material from the cultures of the groups they wish to represent in order to protect their well-being or to gain political advantage.[42] For the DPP, portraying the Taiwanese as the "host" group is a powerful means of attacking the ruling KMT, especially nonmainstream politicians. For the mainstream faction within the KMT, labeling nonmainstream mainlander politicians as "traitors to Taiwan" is a direct way to mobilize public opinion against conservative policies. On this point, the mainstream faction and the DPP find a common enemy. Both the ruling and opposition parties have utilized ethnicity as a tool in the struggle for power. This subethnic factor penetrates into the bureaucracy and social life and leads to unnecessary bureaucratic infighting and social conflicts.

Conclusion

Taiwan's democratization is neither a top-down nor a bottom-up revolution. No single force has been able to determine the outcome of democratization, and the unexpected consequence has been cooperation between the state and society.

This type of democratization has created new actors in policymaking. Within the state hierarchy, factional conflicts have divided the once-coherent elite group and led to a fierce power struggle. In these circumstances, policy outcome is always the result of compromise among competing groups. On the other hand, social forces also get the chance to participate in the policymaking process through a variety of alliances with the state elite.

Elite endeavors during the process of democratization have had a substantial impact on Taiwan's China policy. Mainstream and nonmainstream factions differ over the tempo and general direction of interaction between the two sides of the Taiwan Straits, and these differences are reflected in bureaucratic conflicts over cross-Straits economic policymaking, that is, between the Mainland Affairs Council (MAC) and the semiofficial Straits Exchange Foundation (SEF). Subethnic factors, the indirect result of the KMT's Taiwanization policy and a side effect of elite conflict, also affect inter-elite cooperation on the issue of China policy.

Civil society in Taiwan regained its momentum after the beginning of liberalization. As the state initiated further democratic reforms, winning elections in order to stay in power became the major goal of the KMT. In these circumstances, the KMT is forced to seek alliances with social forces, especially big-business groups, to procure necessary financial support. Moreover, the development of the market has weakened the economic monopoly of the state and created a strong middle class, which demands more political rights and is prepared to protest against unreasonable state policies. Owners of numerous small enterprises, who are the core of Taiwan's middle class, have ignored the state's prohibition and rushed into the booming China market. The ascendance of influential big business groups and autonomous small enterprises is having a major impact on the state's management of cross-Straits economic interaction.

To sum up, democratization has changed state-society interaction in Taiwan. It has led to the division of the political elite, the rise of civil society, and the formation of a variety of state-society alliances. It has also influenced state capacity and state autonomy in controlling social interests and the market mechanism. The crucial impact of this change on the state's management of cross-Straits economic interaction will be discussed in the following chapters.

Notes

1. Herbert Kitschelt, "Political Regime Change: Structure and Process-Driven Explanations," *American Political Science Review* 186, no. 4 (December 1992):1028–1035; Doh Chull Shin, "On the Third Wave of Democratization," *World Politics* 47, no. 1 (October 1994):135–170; Metin Heper, "Transition to Democracy Reconsidered," in *Comparative Political Dynamics*, ed. Dankwart Rustow and Kenneth Erickson (New York: HarperCollins, 1991), 192–211.

2. For structural factors leading to democratization, see Guillermo O'Donnell and Philippe Schmitter, *Transitions from Authoritarian Rule: Tentative Conclusions About Uncertain Democracies* (Baltimore: Johns Hopkins University Press, 1986); Samuel Huntington, "Will More Countries Become Democratic," *Political Science Quarterly* 99, no. 2 (Summer 1984):193–218; Samuel Huntington, *The Third Wave:*

Democratization in the Late Twentieth Century (Norman: University of Oklahoma Press, 1991).

3. Charles Lindblom, *Democracy and Market System* (Oslo: Norwegian University Press, 1988), 44–54.

4. Robert Dahl, *Democracy and Its Critics* (New Haven: Yale University Press, 1989), chapter 17.

5. Barrington Moore, *The Social Origins of Dictatorship and Democracy* (Harmondsworth, England: Penguin, 1966).

6. Dietrick Ruseschemeyer, Evelyne Huber Stephens, and John Stephens disagree with Moore and argue that it is not the "commercial bourgeoisie" but the working class allying with middle-class mobilization that contributes to the emergence of democracy. See their *Capitalist Development and Democracy* (Chicago: University of Chicago Press, 1992).

7. John Keane, *Democracy and Civil Society* (London: Verso Press, 1988), 14.

8. Juan Linz, "Transitions to Democracy," *Washington Quarterly* 13, no. 3 (Summer 1990):143–164.

9. O'Donnell and Schmitter, *Transitions from Authoritarian Rule*, chapter 2.

10. Adam Przeworski, *Democracy and the Market* (Cambridge: Cambridge University Press, 1991), 57.

11. Huntington, *The Third Wave*, chapter 3.

12. Samuel Huntington, *Political Order in Changing Societies* (New Haven: Yale University Press, 1968).

13. Alfred Stepan, *Rethinking Military Politics: Brazil and the Southern Cone* (Princeton: Princeton University Press, 1988), 4.

14. Giuseppe Di Palma, *To Craft Democracies* (Berkeley: University of California Press, 1990), 44.

15. Parris Chang, "The Changing Nature of Taiwan's Politics," in *Taiwan: Beyond the Economic Miracle*, ed. Denis Fred Simon and Michael Y. M. Kau (New York: M. E. Sharpe, 1992), 30.

16. Hung-mao Tien, *The Great Transition: Political and Social Change in the Republic of China* (Stanford: Stanford University Press, 1989), 185.

17. Andrew Nathan and Helena Ho, "Chiang Ching-kuo's Decision for Political Reform," in *Chiang Ching-kuo's Leadership in the Development of the Republic of China on Taiwan*, ed. Shao-chuan Leng (Lanham, Maryland: University Press of America, 1993), 42.

18. *Zili wanbao* (Independence Evening News), March 6, 1989.

19. For a detailed discussion of the split in the KMT, see Wang Li-hsin, *Wukui— Hao Bocun de zhengzhi zhi lu* (Political Life of Hau Pei-tsun) (Taipei: Tien-hsia, 1994); Chou Yu-kou, *Li Denghui diyi qiantian* (The first thousand days of Lee Teng-hui) (Taipei: Mai Tien, 1993).

20. Yu-shan Wu, "Nationalism, Democratization and Economic Reform: Political Transition in the Soviet Union, Hungary, and Taiwan," Working Papers in Taiwan Studies, Conference Group of Taiwan Studies (USA), no. 2, 1995, 39.

21. Antonio Gramsci, *Selections From the Prison Notebooks*, ed. Quintin Hoare and Geoffrey Smith (New York: International Publishers, 1971).

22. Huang, Teh-fu, *Minzhu jingbudang yu Taiwan diqu zhengzhi minzhuhua* (The Democratic Progressive Party and Taiwan's Democratization) (Taipei: Shih-ying, 1992), chapter 3.

23. Lu Ya-li, "Political Opposition in Taiwan," in *Political Changes in Taiwan*, ed. Tun-jen Cheng and Stephan Haggard (Boulder: Lynne Rienner, 1992), 140.

24. Chang Chun-hung, *Dao zhizheng zhi lu: Difang baowei zhongyang zhi lilun yu shiji* (The Road to Power: Theory and Practice of Encircling the Center from the Periphery) (Taipei: Nan-fang, 1989). Chang is one of the most important strategists of the Formosa faction.

25. Przeworski, *Democracy and the Market*, 11.

26. Lee Kuo-hsiung, "The Politics of ROC's Constitutional Reform" (paper presented at the 36th annual meeting of the American Political Science Association, Washington, D.C., September 2–5, 1993), 19.

27. Chou, *Li Denghui diyi qiantian*, 208.

28. Lee Teng-hui, "Inaugural Address of the Eighth-Term President," in *Creating the Future* (Taipei: Government Information Office, 1992), 5.

29. Hungdah Chiu, "Constitutional Development and Reform in the Republic of China in Taiwan," *Issues & Studies* 29, no. 1 (January 1993):24.

30. Ramon Myers, "The First Chinese Democracy," in *Quiet Revolution*, ed. Jason Hu (Taipei: Government Information Office, 1994), p. 45.

31. Chiu, "Constitutional Development and Reform," 26.

32. Ouyang Jen, "ROC's Constitutional Reform, 1990–1992" (master's thesis, National Chengchi University, 1994), 80–83.

33. Lee, "The Politics of ROC's Constitutional Reform," 22.

34. *Lianhe bao* (United Daily News), April 19, 1991.

35. Shao-chuan Leng and Cheng-yi Lin, "Political Change on Taiwan: Transition to Democracy?" *China Quarterly*, no. 136 (December 1993):813–814.

36. Lee, "The Politics of ROC's Constitutional Reform," 24.

37. Jurgen Domes, "Taiwan in 1992," *Asian Survey* 33, no. 1 (January 1993):58.

38. Ouyang, "ROC's Constitutional Reform," 128.

39. *Shibao zhoukan* (China Times Weekly), February 7, 1993, 8–14.

40. Hung-mao Tien, "Taiwan's Parliamentary Election and Cabinet Reshuffling" (paper delivered at the Sino-American Conference on Contemporary China, Washington, D.C., June 20–22, 1993), 13.

41. *Shibao zhoukan*, August 28, 1993, 28.

42. Paul Brass, *Ethnic Groups and the State* (Totowa, N.J.: Barnes and Noble, 1985), chapter 2.

3

An Overview of Taiwan's China Policy

This chapter will discuss the general trend of Taiwan's policy toward China. After analyzing democratic transition in Taiwan, it is perceived that new actors—hardliners, reformers, and the opposition party—have emerged to influence the policymaking process. Democratization has released social forces and incorporated opposition forces into the institutional framework. In contrast to policymaking during the authoritarian era, voices from the opposition camp and the general public are having an increasing impact on state actions.

Beijing is also playing an important role by pressuring Taipei to stick to a "one China" policy rather than to set itself up as a rival Chinese regime or to openly pursue independence. Moreover, interaction between the two sides of the Taiwan Straits is partially a reflection of the current international system. After the normalization of Sino-American relations in 1979, Taiwan failed to take the initiative in promoting its relations with China. Taiwan's passive policy at that time was a reaction to increasing pressure from the PRC's proposals for the peaceful unification of China.

In the following pages, it is argued that Taiwan's China policy is not formed by autonomous actions initiated by the state elite. Instead, it is a compromise between KMT and opposition forces and between unification and independence. This chapter will also discuss the evolution of the PRC's national unification policy and analyze the DPP's proposals for Taiwan independence. Finally, it will be explained how the Taiwanese state responds to pressure from the PRC and how it accommodates the issues of national identity, national security, and national unification. All these have an important impact on Taiwan's economic policies toward China.

The PRC's Unification Policy

The PRC's original policy of national unification was to "liberate" Taiwan by military force. In the 1950s and 1960s Beijing continuously threatened to use force against Taiwan and at times shelled the small Nationalist-occupied islands close to the Chinese coast, notably in 1954 and 1958. The PRC also condemned U.S. interference in China's "domestic affairs." During this period, Beijing asserted that in order to preserve the integrity of Chinese territory, it would utilize all possible means, including military force, to liberate Taiwan from foreign control.[1] In this sense, the military strife between the two sides of the Taiwan Straits was a reflection of the international system of bipolar confrontation during the Cold War era.

While keeping up its military threat, the PRC also launched a campaign for "peaceful liberation" through political means. At a meeting of the National People's Congress (NPC) in 1956, Premier Zhou Enlai pledged that "the Chinese people will seek to liberate Taiwan by peaceful means as far as it is possible," adding that "the possibility of peaceful liberation is increasing." Zhou declared that the PRC was willing to negotiate with the Taiwan authorities specific steps and terms for the peaceful liberation of Taiwan and urged that representatives be sent to Beijing or some other suitable location to carry out such negotiation.[2]

The PRC's two-track liberation policy was not changed until the system of bipolar confrontation was eased and relations improved between Beijing and Washington. Making a virtue out of necessity in order to reach a compromise with the United States, the PRC adopted a conciliatory policy toward Taiwan following the normalization of relations in 1979. The peaceful reunification policy was a tacit quid pro quo for the U.S. action, and an indication that the Chinese did not intend to take advantage of Taiwan's new military vulnerability. Beijing also promptly announced a halt to the regular shelling of the offshore islands.[3]

The Chinese Communist Party (CCP) made it clear that it had adopted a policy of "peaceful reunification" rather than "armed liberation" with respect to Taiwan at the Third Plenum of its Eleventh Central Committee in December 1978. This policy included proposals for consultations and negotiations on an equal footing between the two sides.[4]

On New Year's Day 1979, the NPC Standing Committee released a "Message to Compatriots in Taiwan" that proposed that military confrontation between Taiwan and China should be ended through bilateral discussions in order to create the conditions for a whole range of contacts and exchanges. The PRC also suggested that all barriers to direct contacts should be eliminated, and that direct trade, postal, and transportation links should be permitted immediately.[5]

The most substantial element of the peaceful reunification proposal was the "one country, two systems" plan, which has served as the basis of Beijing's policy toward Taiwan since the early 1980s. This formula appeared first in a nine-point statement issued by Ye Jianying, chairman of the NPC Standing Committee, in 1981, and it was taken up again by Deng Xiaoping in a 1984 speech about China's unification.[6] From then on, with some variations, this formula remained the mainstay of Beijing's unification policy.

The "one country, two systems" formula allows for the coexistence of socialism and capitalism within a united China. As a special administrative region of the PRC, Taiwan would be permitted a high level of autonomy, including independent executive, legislative, and judicial powers, and its own armed forces. Representatives from Taiwan would also be allowed to participate in the central government in Beijing. However, the government in Taipei would be relegated to the status of a local authority and its exercise of autonomy would never be allowed to conflict with the policies of the central government. Unification according to this formula would be conducted through negotiations between the ruling parties, rather than the governments, on the two sides of the Taiwan Straits.[7] In brief, under the "one country, two systems" formula, Taiwan would be an autonomous political entity, but its status would not be equal to that of the PRC, which would be the sole legitimate representative of China in the international arena.

For the time being, Beijing demands that Taiwan lift all barriers to cross-Straits interaction; direct trade, postal, and telecommunications links, and direct negotiations between Taiwan and China should be initiated immediately. On the other hand, Beijing still reserves the right to achieve unification through military force, though in a restricted set of extreme circumstances. These circumstances are: (1) if Taiwan declares independence; (2) if there is any foreign interference in Taiwan's domestic affairs; (3) if domestic turmoil breaks out on the island; or (4) if Taiwan persists in refusing to negotiate for a long period of time.[8] Hence, under the assumption that there is only "one China," the PRC applies both the carrot and the stick in its dealings with Taiwan. While providing preferential treatment to Taiwan investors in order to persuade Taipei to permit further interaction, it also refuses to give up the option of using force as a warning to supporters of independence.

After Taiwan launched its democratic reforms in the late 1980s, Beijing, while keeping its "one China" policy as the bottom line, also introduced some more flexible elements. In an interview with the Taiwan newspaper *Zhongguo shibao* (China Times) on September 24, 1990, PRC President Yang Shangkun rejected the idea of a "nonaggression treaty" with

Taiwan, asserting that "if we sign the treaty, it would mean that we recognized Taiwan as a sovereign state. It is absolutely impossible for us to hold state-to-state negotiations with Taiwan. China has only one government, and this government is located in Beijing."[9] But on a more flexible note, Wang Zhaoguo, director of the PRC State Council's Taiwan Affairs Office, indicated on June 6, 1991 that the PRC's threat to use force was not directed at the Taiwanese people but at potential foreign intervention and the Taiwan independence movement. Wang also applauded the KMT's insistence on a "one China" policy and invited all the political forces and political parties to discuss any issue concerning Taiwan.[10] According to later explanations from Beijing, "any issue concerning Taiwan" included Taiwan's status in international organizations.[11] CCP general secretary Jiang Zemin adopted a similar tone in his speech at the CCP's Fourteenth National Congress in 1992. Jiang stated that under the condition that there was only one China, Beijing was willing to discuss whatever questions Taipei wanted. In this speech, Jiang did not mention the issue of using force against Taiwan.[12]

Wang Zhaoguo's speech in 1991 was a response to Taiwan's termination of the "mobilization period," while Jiang's in 1992 paved the way for the Koo-Wang talks, the historic meeting in April 1993 between the heads of the quasi-official negotiating bodies on the two sides: Koo Chen-fu of Taipei's Straits Exchange Foundation and Wang Daohan of Beijing's Association for Relations Across the Taiwan Straits (ARATS). However, due to the ongoing restructuring of power within the state and the KMT's efforts to adjust to the issue of Taiwan independence, Taipei did not make any immediate positive response to the PRC's more flexible line.

In August 1993, Beijing issued an important policy white paper entitled "The Taiwan Question and Reunification of China." The timing of this document was very significant. In Taiwan, the opposition DPP had achieved a breakthrough in its electoral performance in the Legislative Yuan elections of December 1992, and the KMT's mainstream faction had consolidated its power after the party's Fourteenth Congress in August 1993. This was the moment when Beijing chose to deliver a message concerning its policy bottom line to the new power holders within and outside the state hierarchy in Taiwan. Also, after the Koo-Wang talks in April 1993, Taipei had begun to promote itself as a political entity on an equal footing with Beijing and to campaign for entry into the United Nations. Beijing's white paper was therefore an effort to deter Taipei from using the "one country, two equal political entities" model to participate in the international community.

In the white paper, Beijing reiterated its policy of peaceful reunification and the "one country, two systems" formula, which it defined as consisting of four elements: one China, the coexistence of two systems, a high degree of autonomy for Taiwan, and negotiations. As expected, Beijing reiterated that it would use all necessary means, including military force, to maintain the integrity of its territory.

Beijing was also fiercely critical of the Taiwan independence movement in the white paper. It claimed that Taipei paid only lip service to national unification and set up various obstacles to impede closer interaction with China. Taipei's negative attitude, it was argued, indirectly encouraged the rise of the Taiwan independence movement. In other words, Beijing was warning both the antiunification faction within the state and the radical Taiwan independence faction in the opposition camp that a declaration of independence would provoke a military response from China.

Furthermore, Beijing also clearly rejected all the formulas put forward by Taipei for Taiwan's participation in international organizations, including "dual recognition," "two Chinas," "one country, two seats," and "one China, one Taiwan." According to the white paper, the PRC is the only representative of China in the United Nations and its related organizations, and Taiwan's participation under the title "Taipei, China" in the Asian Development Bank (ADB) and "Chinese Taipei" in the Asia-Pacific Economic Cooperation forum is entirely the result of an agreement between the PRC and other member states, and this model cannot be applied to other intergovernmental organizations. As for nongovernmental organizations, Taiwan's participation also requires the consent of the PRC, and the titles "Taipei, China" or "Taiwan, China" are permissible in this case because they reflect Taiwan's status as a province of the PRC.[13]

Jiang Zemin's eight-point statement on relations with Taiwan, delivered on January 30, 1995, reiterated the PRC's basic guidelines for reunification.[14] These eight points were: (1) the "one China" policy as the basis of peaceful reunification and opposition to any departure from this principle, such as an "independent Taiwan," "two Chinas over a certain period of time," or "split the country and rule under separate regimes"; (2) allowing Taiwan, on condition that it abides by the "one China" principle, to develop cultural and economic relations with other countries; (3) negotiations to end confrontation and to promote reunification; (4) an assurance that the threat to use force is directed at foreign forces and advocates of "Taiwan independence," not at the general public in Taiwan; (5) desire to promote economic cooperation between the two sides and avoid politics interfering with economic affairs; (6) Chinese culture as the basis of China's reunification; (7) full respect for Taiwan compatriots' desire for autonomy; (8) an open invitation for Taiwan leaders to visit China and willingness to accept an invitation to visit Taiwan, because these meetings should not take place in an international setting.

In brief, Beijing's Taiwan policy is in reality a policy of reunification. From Beijing's perspective, China's sovereignty resides in the PRC, and

Taiwan can only enjoy some degree of autonomy in domestic affairs. Since Taiwan is a province of China, it can participate in the international arena only as a local government. Beijing's strategy is to press Taipei to open up people-to-people interaction and initiate a political dialogue with China while at the same time vetoing Taiwan's participation as a full-fledged political entity in all international organizations. These "peaceful means" are adopted in the hope that they will narrow Taiwan's options and give it no choice but to negotiate for reunification. The PRC reserves the right to use force if these peaceful means fail.

The baseline of Beijing's policy toward Taiwan is the "one China" principle. In Beijing's eyes, President Lee Teng-hui's visit to the United States in June 1995 destroyed the international consensus on "one China," and the Chinese had therefore no choice but to take action. In July 1995, Beijing launched a series of unprecedented attacks upon Lee. In four commentaries published jointly by the *Renmin ribao* (People's Daily) and the Xinhua News Agency, China accused Lee of "destroying cross-Straits relations." Lee's efforts to expand Taiwan's international ties through "pragmatic diplomacy" are regarded as nothing more than "Taiwan independence" in disguise. According to Beijing's propaganda machine, Lee is trying to give the "Republic of China on Taiwan" an international identity by creating "two Chinas," or "one China, one Taiwan," or seeking international recognition of an independent Taiwan.[15] Beijing followed up this propaganda campaign with missile tests in waters close to Taiwan and canceled all talks between the SEF and ARATS, including the second Koo-Wang talks scheduled for summer 1995. Cross-Straits relations reached a new low at that time.

The DPP's China Policy

The main theme of the opposition DPP's China policy is that Taiwan needs to end the "confrontational stalemate" with China and develop a "stable and equal framework" of cross-Straits relations. In contrast to the KMT, the DPP regards cross-Straits relations as a state-to-state relationship and believes that Taiwan's China policy should be an extension of its foreign policy.

The DPP's policy is based on the assumption that Taiwan will become independent. In the early stages of the democratization process, the DPP was careful to make sure that its advocation of independence kept just inside the law. In early 1988, the party released its first formal document on Taiwan independence, "Resolution 417," which set out four situations in which Taiwan should declare independence: (1) if the KMT consents to party-to-party negotiations with the CCP; (2) if the KMT sells out Taiwan; (3) if the PRC seeks to unify China by force; and (4) if the KMT refuses democratic reforms.[16] At this stage, Taiwan independence was used by the DPP as an instrument to press the KMT toward reform, and the document was really a trial balloon used to test public and KMT party-state reaction.

After the split within the KMT between the mainstream and nonmainstream factions in 1990, the DPP began to promote the idea of Taiwan's independent sovereignty. In "Resolution 1017 on the Sovereignty of Taiwan" and the "Principles of Cross-Straits Relations," the DPP argued that the ROC's sovereignty does not extend to territory controlled by the PRC or to Mongolia. The ROC's sovereignty is limited to the Taiwan area, and all the government's domestic and foreign policies should be based on this fundamental assumption.[17] As Chen Chung-hsin, director of the DPP's Policy Research Department, has indicated, the timing of these statements about the sovereignty issue was important. They were directed against the "unrealistic fantasy of unification" that ultraconservative elements within the KMT were promoting. The DPP was also delivering a signal to liberals within the KMT and the general public that it was meaningless to engage in debate about unification at that stage. The most urgent task was to deal with substantive problems in cross-Straits interaction through dialogue, conciliation, and negotiation.[18]

At this stage, the DPP's China policy was not based on Taiwan independence. In early 1991, Chen Shui-bian, at that time a DPP legislator, was advocating the signing of a cross-Straits peace treaty between the PRC and the ROC (not "Taiwan"). In other words, before 1992 the DPP followed a "two Chinas" policy; it recognized that the PRC had effective control over China but considered that Taiwan's sovereignty was separate from that of the PRC.[19] It was not until the DPP's Fifth Congress in October 1991 that the party unequivocally adopted a proindependence stance.

The actions of the Fifth Congress were largely a reaction to the first stage of constitutional revision undertaken by the unreformed National Assembly. Furthermore, the DPP was preparing for the first comprehensive National Assembly election scheduled for December that year. The party saw the independence cause as a way of mobilizing public, especially native Taiwanese, support at the polls, and thereby enabling it to influence the second stage of constitutional revision. The main resolutions at the congress concerning Taiwan independence were:

1. Taiwan's sovereignty is separate from the PRC's—this is a historical reality recognized by the international community.
2. Taiwan should establish itself as a new nation, initiate a new constitution, and return to the international arena under its own name.
3. Taiwan should redefine its territory and establish diplomatic relations with the PRC according to international law.

4. Based on the principle of popular sovereignty, a plebiscite should
    be held to decide whether Taiwan should declare independence
    and initiate a new constitution.[20]

The second of these resolutions—qualified by the fourth—was then
included in the DPP's party platform. The Fifth Congress was a turning
point in the development of the DPP in general and its China policy in
particular. After the return to Taiwan of dissidents driven into exile under
the Chiang regime, the radical New Tide faction reached a balance of
power with the moderate Formosa faction. The inclusion of the "independence clause" in the party platform at this congress reflected the new
power structure of the DPP. However, the "popular sovereignty" resolution also implied that although Taiwan independence was the DPP's ultimate goal, an independent Taiwan would not necessarily come about
even if the DPP became the ruling party. The DPP was willing to play by
the democratic rules, and a declaration of independence would depend
on the results of a plebiscite. Furthermore, moderate factions within the
DPP argued that the inclusion of the "independence clause" was aimed at
promoting debate on the issue of Taiwan independence. The goal of the
DPP was to rally public support so that Taiwan's future would be decided at the ballot box rather than by mass movements.[21]

Taiwan independence was the DPP's reason for existence. However, the
independence clause is a political declaration, not a substantial policy outline. It does not suggest any policy agenda, process, or priorities for managing Taiwan's relations with China. The DPP's poor performance in the
1991 National Assembly election showed that the public had little confidence in the independence cause.

Finally, at the end of 1992, the DPP released its first China policy white
paper. Chapter 10 of the white paper—which is entitled "The DPP's *China*
Policy," rather than "mainland" policy, the term used by the KMT—sets
out the party's policy toward China based on Taiwan independence.
Besides repeating Resolution 417 and the resolutions of the Fifth
Congress, the white paper goes one step further by recognizing the PRC
as the only legitimate government of China. It states that the DPP opposes any kind of political negotiations with the PRC before the ending of
hostilities on any secret deals between the KMT and the CCP. The white
paper claims that Taiwan should base its relations with the PRC on the
"one China" principle; negotiations between Taiwan and China should
adopt a government-to-government format and should follow the practice of international law.[22]

The DPP's breakthrough in the 1992 Legislative Yuan election made it a
"determinant minority" in the legislature. Having gained 31.86 percent of
the popular vote, the DPP enjoyed veto power on some crucial public policy issues. The opposition party's success at the polls also encouraged it

to adjust its role from that of a dissident to a participant in the formulation of the government's China policy. In the 1995 Legislative Yuan election, the DPP gained 33.17 percent of the popular vote, an increase of 1.31 percentage points over 1992.[23] The defeat of some radical advocates of Taiwan independence delivered a signal to the DPP that in order to achieve its goal of becoming the ruling party, it must pay more attention to public policy and play the role of a parliamentary party instead of a mass movement.

From the DPP's perspective, Taiwan has been independent since 1949, and its policy statements simply legitimize the status quo. The party is opposed to the KMT's "one China" policy, arguing that it will lead to Taiwan's final incorporation into the PRC. Hence, the DPP has asserted that "Taiwan is Taiwan, China is China," and that Taiwan's relations with China must be based on the principles of equality, mutual benefit, and stability.[24] To ensure peaceful bilateral relations, the PRC must abandon its threat to use force against Taiwan and Taiwan must withdraw its troops from Quemoy and Matsu. The ultimate goal is a nonaggression treaty between the two states. Under peaceful conditions, cultural, economic, and social interaction between Taiwan and China should be encouraged.[25]

The DPP is more prudent in its attitude toward economic interaction between Taiwan and China. Within the DPP hierarchy, the moderate and more radical factions differ on the pace of economic interaction, but the consensus within the party is that economic policies must be kept separate from the sovereignty issue, and a closer economic relationship is a good thing provided Taiwan's national security and general economic interests are guaranteed. The DPP believes that the government should allow the market mechanism to regulate economic interaction, but it is opposed to the establishment of a "Greater China" economic entity. By the same token, the DPP also opposes what it sees as unrealistic attempts to use Taiwan's economic influence to change China's political system.[26]

To sum up, as the DPP gradually increased its political influence through elections, support for Taiwan independence gained political momentum in society. To attract public support and votes, the ruling party had to revise its unification policy and find a gray area between unification and independence. The role the DPP played in this process was that of raising the public's consciousness of Taiwan's uniqueness and autonomy and then pressing the state to be cautious in its handling of cross-Straits relations.

Taiwan's Official China Policy

After its defeat in the civil war on the Chinese mainland, the ROC government retreated to Taiwan, which it sought to use as a military base for

the "recovery" of China. Chiang Kai-shek rejected all proposals for negotiation emanating from China and declared that there was "absolutely no
possibility of any compromise" with the CCP regime since "the Chinese
Government has already had too many painful experiences in negotiating
with the Communists."[27] After the normalization of relations between the
PRC and the United States and the release of the "Message to Compatriots
in Taiwan" on New Year's Day 1979, military confrontation between the
two sides of the Taiwan Straits was transformed into peaceful coexistence.
However, Taipei regarded the PRC's conciliatory posture as a "united
front tactic" aimed at undermining Taiwan's resistance. It continued to
reject flatly PRC proposals to negotiate, to open direct trade, or to establish postal, shipping, or civil aviation links. The manifesto of the Twelfth
National Congress of the KMT in 1981 reiterated the KMT's unyielding
anti-Communist position and declared that the party was determined to
unify China under Sun Yat-sen's Three Principles of the People. The manifesto warned: "We know that to talk peace with the enemy amounts to
inviting our own collapse and that to compromise with the enemy is the
same as destroying ourselves."[28]

Significant policy change was not realized until 1987, when Chiang
Ching-kuo decided to legalize indirect trade and transportation links
with China. Knowing that his health was declining and aware of rising
demands for a change of policy within society, Chiang adopted a bold
policy of domestic liberalization and an opening up of interaction with
China. Although direct links were still prohibited and the "three nos"
policy (no official contacts, no negotiations, and no compromise)
remained unchanged, Chiang's initiatives began a new era in Taiwan's
China policy.

Taiwan's policy toward China since 1988 may be divided into two periods. Between Lee Teng-hui's accession to the presidency in January 1988
until the resignation of Premier Hau Pei-tsun in February 1993, Taiwan's
China policy was an amalgamation of the views of the KMT nonmainstream faction's hardline stance, the DPP's Taiwan independence policy,
and the mainstream faction's more flexible approach to unification. By the
end of 1992, Lee had begun to consolidate his power, and from the time of
Hau's resignation the mainstream faction dominated Taiwan's China policy. Throughout both periods, Beijing has tried to deter the DPP and the
KMT mainstream faction from discarding the "one China" principle.

In the early days of Lee's presidency, the government adhered to
Chiang Ching-kuo's "three nos" policy but tried to get around the edges
of this framework and seek a breakthrough in relations with China. In his
1990 inaugural address, Lee announced three preconditions for a complete opening up of economic, trade, academic, cultural, and scientific
exchange with China:

1. Recognition by Beijing of the overall world trend toward democracy and the common hope of all Chinese.
2. Implementation of political democracy and a free economic system in China.
3. Renunciation of the threat to use military force against Taiwan and an undertaking not to interfere with Taiwan's development of its foreign relations on the basis of the one-China policy.[29]

These three preconditions were unacceptable to China because they required a fundamental change in the principles of Communist rule. However, at a press conference two days later, President Lee stated that "it is not necessary that all three conditions I put forward are met before we can improve relations with China." Rather, he said, "issues can be dealt with one by one."[30] It was obvious that Lee had reiterated the usual anticommunist clichés to please the still-powerful conservative factions within the state while at the same time trying to achieve some breakthrough with the Chinese. He was indicating that this breakthrough should be based on the principle of political equality and Taiwan's autonomy instead of unification at any cost.

From early 1991 to late 1992, the two main factions of the KMT clashed repeatedly on the issue of the party's China policy. At around the same time, the DPP inserted the Taiwan independence clause into its party constitution. Within the KMT camp, the nonmainstream faction favored broader economic and cultural exchange across the Straits and the creation of a "Greater China Economic Circle." The mainstream faction, on the other hand, insisted that the ban on direct transportation should only be lifted on condition that Beijing recognize Taiwan as an equal political entity and renounce the option of using force to settle the reunification issue. To the nonmainstream faction, China's unification was the ultimate goal, and proponents of Taiwan independence were labeled as secessionists and the government was urged to take legal action against them. The mainstream faction, on the other hand, pushed steadily for the removal of legal restrictions on the promotion of independence. The issue of direct election of the president was also used by nonmainstreamers to attack what they saw as their rivals' departure from the "one China" principle. They argued that the direct election of the president by the Taiwanese people alone would imply the abandonment of the ROC's reunification goal.[31]

The "Guidelines for National Unification" promulgated in March 1991 was, in one sense, a compromise between these two forces within the state. The very title of the "Guidelines" implied that the government was committed to the one-China policy and that national unification was its ultimate goal. However, the "Guidelines" also insisted that unification would have to be preceded by "an appropriate period of forthright exchange, cooperation and consultation conducted on the principles of reason, peace, equality and reciprocity."[32]

The "Guidelines" adopted a three-phase program for unification. In the first phase, the aim is to increase people-to-people exchanges in order to enhance understanding and respect between the two sides of the Taiwan Straits and thus reduce hostility. Each side should renounce the right to use force against the other and recognize the other as an equal political entity. In the second phase, as mutual trust and cooperation increase, bilateral governmental contacts should be established. Direct postal, transportation, and commercial links are to be permitted, and a joint venture to develop the southeastern coastal area of China will be initiated. Exchanges of visits by high-ranking officials on both sides should be encouraged in order to create favorable conditions for consultation and unification. In the final phase, an institution should be established jointly by the two sides to facilitate discussions leading to the creation of a democratic, free, and equitably prosperous China.[33]

The important thing about the "Guidelines" is that it confirms that under the one-China principle, the ROC and the PRC are political entities enjoying equal status. Moreover, it gives no fixed timetable for unification: The length of each phase depends entirely on how long it takes to achieve its goals. However, the "Guidelines" does not provide a definition of "one China." If the two political entities are equal, "China" could refer to the People's Republic of China, the Republic of China, or some kind of special arrangement prior to unification.

This ambiguity aroused doubts among both the Chinese and the DPP. While Beijing condemned Taipei's attempt to create "two governments under the guise of one China," the DPP argued that unification on these terms would lead to the incorporation of Taiwan into the PRC. With Legislative Yuan elections due in December 1992, the KMT's China policy came under increasing attack from the DPP for its failure to dispel fears that unification would simply be a betrayal of Taiwan.

In August 1992, the National Unification Council (NUC) finally issued a definition of "one China." It stated that Taipei considered "one China" to mean the Republic of China founded in 1911 with de jure sovereignty over all of China. The ROC, it continued, currently has jurisdiction only over Taiwan, Penghu, Kinmen, and Matsu. Taiwan is part of China, and the Chinese mainland is part of China as well. Since 1949, China has been temporarily divided, and each side of the Taiwan Straits is administered by a separate political entity.[34]

This document inhabits the gray area between Taiwan independence and unification. Its most important points are, first, that Taiwan and China are equal political entities, and second, that these two entities have separate titles and spheres of jurisdiction. Instead of declaring that Taiwan and China are two separate sovereign states, the document argues that the sovereignty of the Republic of China overlaps that of the People's Republic of China: Taipei and Beijing share China's sovereignty. According to the NUC's definition, "one China" is a cultural and historical concept.

The "one China, two political entities" formula helped to increase the legitimacy of the "Republic of China on Taiwan."[35] As Taiwan's democratization gradually went on track and the sense of an autonomous Taiwan outside of PRC control grew stronger on the island, the regime needed a new kind of legitimacy to be used to promote national cohesion and consensus. The "two political entities" formula satisfied this need. The formula seemed to have all the advantages of the DPP's independence policy without the danger to Taiwan's security that an out-and-out declaration of independence would incur.

The government did not come up with any substantial policies based on "one China, two political entities" until after Hau Pei-tsun's resignation as premier in February 1993. From 1988 to 1992, Lee Teng-hui used the appeal of "democracy" to fight conservative forces within the state; from 1992 up to the present, Lee has been using democracy to combat China's policy of unification under "one country, two systems."

Lee first mentioned the idea that the people of Taiwan had formed a *shengming gongtongti* (usually rendered as gemeinschaft or "common destiny") in his keynote speech at the third meeting of the Second National Assembly in April 1993. Different opinions concerning Taiwan's China policy, he said, could be dealt with through democratic channels, and the policy itself must be based on a consensus of all groups in society.[36] Lee elaborated on this idea a couple of months later, emphasizing that in a pluralistic, democratic society, this consensus is the only thing Taiwan can rely on to help meet the threat from outside.[37]

Thus, Lee Teng-hui used public opinion and the idea of a "national consensus" in Taiwan to strengthen the ROC's legitimacy as a political entity separate from PRC control and to resist the PRC's insistence that it was the repository of China's sovereignty. At a press conference during an official visit to Latin America in May 1994, Lee said: "The Chinese Communist regime says China's sovereignty is in its hands. I say, sorry, China's sovereignty is in the hands of all the Chinese people, including people in Taiwan. Since democratization, Taiwan's sovereignty has been in the hands of the Taiwanese people, not the PRC. The PRC is not qualified to declare Taiwan's sovereignty."[38]

Lee Teng-hui's diplomatic and China policy initiatives since mid-1993 have been supported by democratization and the Taiwanese people's desire for autonomy and quest for survival. Only one-fourth of the

TABLE 3.1   Public Opinion Polls on Independence and Unification
(in percentages)

	June 1989	Jan. 1991	Dec. 1991	June 1992	June 1993	Dec. 1994	July 1995
Unification	20.5	31.3	27.2	29.9	20.8	22.6	20.0
Independence	2.1	3.6	3.2	6.4	–	11.7	14.0
Status Quo	57.5	45.0	42.8	41.6	43.1	43.3	46.0
No Comment	19.7	20.1	26.3	22.2	–	23.4	20.0

SOURCE: *Opinion Poll Data* (Taipei: Mainland Affairs Council, August 1993 and August 1995);
Lienhe bao (United Daily News), June 30, 1993.

Taiwanese people want unification, and the majority prefer the status quo
(see Table 3.1). Taiwan has used the concept of "popular sovereignty" to
resist the PRC's insistence that it is the repository of China's—and
Taiwan's—sovereignty. Lee's ideas about popular sovereignty and
gemeinschaft were incorporated into "Relations Across the Taiwan
Straits," Taipei's China policy white paper released in July 1994. Although
reconfirming Taiwan's "one China, two political entities" framework, this
document to some degree redefined the meaning of "political entity." It
says: "The meaning of the term 'political entity' is quite broad; it can be
applied to a state, a government, or a political organization. Only when
both sides of the Taiwan Straits set aside the 'sovereignty dispute' for the
time being will we untangle the knots that have bound us for the past
forty years or more and progress smoothly toward unification. The concept of a 'political entity' will help us loosen those knots."[39]
    In contrast to the "Guidelines for National Unification" and the NUC's
1992 declaration on the meaning of "one China," the white paper did not
attempt to enter the debate over which entity, the PRC or the ROC, was
the rightful repository of China's sovereignty. It focused instead on the
ROC's "equal status" with the PRC. Domestically, the PRC and the ROC
had jurisdiction over their respective territories; internationally, they
should coexist as legal entities in the international arena. Also, for the first
time, the white paper clearly indicated that "unification" and "separation" are two important trends in Taiwan's domestic politics, and that
Taiwan's future will depend on which of these trends gains most public
support:

> We have to admit that Taiwan is a democratic country, with complete free-
> dom of speech and thought, which has inevitably been influenced by both
> integrationist and separatist ideas. Subjectively speaking, the ROC govern-
> ment believes that we should work toward integration, but in objective
> terms, the degree of acceptance which these two trends enjoy among the peo-
> ple will depend on the future development of relations between the two
> sides of the Taiwan Straits. If cross-Straits relations do not develop favorably,

the shadow of separatism is not likely to be dispelled and may indeed grow darker still in Taiwan.[40]

To sum up, from the "three nos" to the white paper, Taiwan's handling of relations with China changed from a stubborn ideological crusade to an acceptance of the PRC as an equal political entity. New policy initiatives since Lee Teng-hui's consolidation of power signify to China that while Taiwan will not declare independence at the current stage, progress in relations across the Taiwan Straits depends on interaction among competing forces in Taiwanese society on the one hand and the PRC's own behavior on the other. The consensus among the people of Taiwan is that Taiwan needs a place in the world arena, and that the PRC should create the conditions for coexistence instead of threatening Taiwan's survival. If the PRC pushes too hard on the issue of Taiwan's autonomy, the chances of achieving unification will be remote. On the "one China" issue, Taipei rejects the PRC's definition that "one China" means the "People's Republic of China." In response to Jiang Zemin's eight-point statement of January 1995, Lee Teng-hui stressed the political reality of China's division under separate governments.[41] Taipei has also adopted a more prudent attitude toward direct transportation and direct trade. Furthermore, in contrast to Beijing's suggestion for immediate political negotiations, Taipei insists that it will negotiate only when Beijing stops threatening to use force against Taiwan.

Conclusion

Taipei's new China policy is not purely a product of the state elite but represents a compromise among various political forces. It is the natural outcome of the democratization process that started in the late 1980s. The rise of the proindependence opposition party has had a major impact on the making of the China policy. Policymakers in the state must resist attacks from prounification conservatives on the one hand and conciliate advocates of independence on the other. Thus, the main goal of Taiwan's China policy has been to seek a gray area between unification and independence. The state is attempting to preserve national security and to develop a peaceful and equal relationship with China at the same time. To avoid accusations of "betrayal" of Taiwan's vital interests, the ruling party has also had to adopt a prudent policy toward trade and investment with China.

Since Taiwan's China policy is the result of a compromise, its goals are ambiguous. The state has failed to reach a consensus about whether the ultimate goal should be independence or unification. Different factions and social forces have their own definitions of Taiwan's core security and economic interests. Moreover, during the fierce power struggle that took place within the KMT from 1990 to 1993, any new policy plan initiated by one faction was liable to meet a stinging attack from rival factions. In this way, conflicts of "high politics" spilled over into the more substantial business of China policy. These disputes also hampered coordination and cooperation between different parts of the bureaucracy.

Taiwan's ambiguous China policy has provoked direct opposition from the other side of the Taiwan Straits. In order to gather electoral support, the ruling KMT has had to stress Taiwan's autonomy and its need to expand the scope of its international activities under the title "Republic of China on Taiwan." From Beijing's perspective, arrangements such as "one China, two political entities" are aimed at bringing about the permanent division of China. The Chinese want Taipei to demonstrate its sincerity by immediately entering into political negotiations and opening direct postal, trade, and transportation links with China. Hence, Lee Teng-hui's visit to the United States in June 1995 was seen by the Chinese as part of his effort to separate Taiwan from China permanently. As a result, cross-Straits relations hit a new low. After China held its retaliatory missile tests, Taiwanese investments in China dropped by approximately 26 percent as businessmen adopted a wait-and-see policy.[42] This heightening of political confrontation has thrown a shadow on cross-Straits economic interaction.

Taiwan's economic policy toward China is closely connected with Taiwan's vital security interests and unification. Whereas prounification forces urge closer economic interaction with China, pro-independence factions prefer a more cautious policy on trade and investment. Differences in policy priorities are not based on cost-benefit analysis. Instead, they are a reflection of competing factional interests and disagreement over the issue of national identity and national development priorities. The result is delay and lack of coordination in policymaking, and a tardy response to economic demands raised by business groups.

Notes

1. See "We Will Certainly Liberate Taiwan," *Renmin ribao* (People's Daily), December 5, 1954; "Struggle for the Liberation of Taiwan," *Renmin ribao*, February 16, 1955. Reprinted in Kuo Li-ming, ed., *Zhonggong duitai zhengce ziliao xuanji, 1949–1991* (Mainland China's Policy Toward Taiwan: Selected Documents, 1949–1991) (Taipei: Yung-yeh, 1992), 102–108, 131–134.

2. Zhou Enlai, "Government Report to the Third Meeting of the National People's Congress," in Kuo, *Zhonggong duitai zhengce ziliao xuanji*, 145–149. For a detailed discussion of the PRC's two-track policy toward Taiwan, see Ralph Clough, "The Republic of China and the World," in *China: Seventy Years After the*

1911 Hsin-Hai Revolution, ed. Hungdah Chiu and Shao-chuan Leng (Charlottesville: University Press of Virginia, 1984), 532–537.

3. For the influence of the U.S. factor in the PRC's policy shift, see Ralph Clough, "The People's Republic of China and the Taiwan Relations Act," in *A Unique Relationship*, ed. Ramon Myers (Stanford: Stanford University Press, 1989), 119–140; Harold Hinton, "The People's Republic of China and the World," in Chiu and Leng, *China*, 457–490.

4. *Beijing Review*, February 3, 1986, 19.

5. *Beijing Review*, January 5, 1979, 17.

6. For the full text of Ye's proposal, see *Beijing Review*, October 5, 1981, 10–11. For Deng's speech, see *Beijing Review*, February 3, 1986, 25–26. See also *Renmin ribao*, October 1, 1981, and January 1, 1985, in Kuo, *Zhonggong duitai zhengce ziliao xuanji*, 412–414, 620–628.

7. *Lianhe bao* (United Daily News) (Taipei), July 27, 1991; John Kuan, "KMT-CCP Negotiations and China's Unification" (paper presented at the annual meeting of the American Political Science Association, Washington, D.C., August 29–September 1, 1991), 20–26; Tzong-ho Bau, "The Essence of Beijing's Policy Toward Taiwan" (paper presented at the annual meeting of the American Political Science Association, September 2–5, 1993), 4.

8. For details of PRC leaders' statements concerning the use of force, see *Zhonggong duitai yongwu kenengxingzhi fenxi* (On the Possibility of the PRC's Using Force Against Taiwan) (Taipei: Government Information Office, 1992).

9. Kuo, *Zhonggong duitai zhengce ziliao xuanji*, 1129–1137.

10. Ibid., 1204–1206.

11. *Shibao zhoukan* (China Times Weekly), April 4, 1993, 32.

12. *Renmin ribao* (Overseas Edition), October 21, 1992.

13. "The Taiwan Question and Reunification of China," *Beijing Review*, September 6–12, 1993, i–viii.

14. Pamphlet issued by the Taiwan Affairs Office, PRC State Council, January 30, 1995.

15. "Lee's Cornell Speech Rapped on Chinese Press," *Beijing Review*, August 14–20, 1995, 12–13.

16. Chen Chung-hsin, "DPP's Mainland Policy and Cross-Straits Relations" (paper presented at the Conference on Cross-Straits Relations, sponsored by the Chinese University of Hong Kong, Hong Kong, July 1992), 10.

17. Hsu Hsin-liang, "Principles of Cross-Straits Relations," December 1990. Cited from *Minzhu jinbudang dalu zhengce jiben wenjian* (Basic Documents of the DPP's Mainland Policy) (Unpublished manuscript, 1994), 116. Hsu Hsin-liang was chairman of the DPP from 1992 to 1994.

18. Chen Chung-hsin, director of the DPP's Policy Research Department, interview with the author, August 20, 1994.

19. *Minzhu jinbudang dalu zhengce*, 180–212.

20. Ibid., 31–32.

21. Chen, "DPP's Mainland Policy," 21.

22. *Minzhu jinbudang zhengce baipishu* (Policy White Paper of the Democratic Progressive Party) (Taipei: DPP Headquarters, August 1993), chapter 10.

23. *Zhongyang ribao* (Central Daily News) (Taipei), December 3, 1995.

24. *Taiwan zhuquan xuanyan* (Declaration of Taiwan's Independent Sovereignty) (Taipei: DPP Headquarters, August, 1994), 11–12.

25. See *Minzhu jinbudang zhengce baipishu*, 231.

26. Chen, interview.

27. Hungdah Chiu, ed., *China and the Question of Taiwan: Documents and Analysis* (New York: Praeger, 1973), 275.

28. Foreign Broadcast Information Service, *Daily Report: China*, April 9, 1981, V3.

29. Lee Teng-hui, "Inaugural Address of the Eighth-Term President," in *Creating the Future* (Taipei: Government Information Office, 1992), 8.

30. Hungdah Chiu, "Koo-Wang Talks and the Prospect of Building Constructive and Stable Relations Across the Taiwan Straits" (paper presented at the Sino-American Conference on Contemporary China, Washington, D.C., June 20–22, 1993), 5.

31. Peng Feng-chen, legislative assistant to Legislator Wang Chien-shien, interview with the author, August 12, 1994. Wang was an active member of the KMT's nonmainstream faction and a founder of the New Party in 1993.

32. *Guidelines for National Unification* (Taipei: Mainland Affairs Council, March 14, 1991).

33. Ibid.

34. *The Meaning of One China* (Taipei: Mainland Affairs Council, August 1992).

35. Milton D. Yeh, "Democratization and Mainland Policy," unpublished manuscript, 1993.

36. *Zhongguo shibao* (China Times), April 10, 1993.

37. Lee Teng-hui, *Speech to the Commencement Ceremony of National Chengchi University* (Taipei: Presidential Office, June 12, 1993), 5.

38. *Zhongguo shibao*, May 7, 1994 and June 1, 1994.

39. *Relations Across the Taiwan Straits* (Taipei: Mainland Affairs Council, 1994), 12.

40. Ibid., 21.

41. Taiwan's official response to Jiang Zemin's eight-point statement may be found in President Lee Teng-hui's speech to the National Unification Council on April 8, 1995. For the full text of Lee's speech, see *Zhongyang ribao*, April 9, 1995.

42. *Ming Pao* (Hong Kong), September 7, 1995.

4

Institutional Conflicts and Power Struggles

In Chapters 2 and 3 it was explained how democratization in Taiwan has led to the division of the political elite and the ascendance of civil society. This chapter will discuss the substantial policymaking capacities of the state, the power structure of the China policy bureaucracy, interagency conflicts, and differences within the elite concerning cross-Straits economic policy.

The study of Taiwan's political economy is dominated by the strong-state paradigm, within which the two prevailing models are the "rationality model" and the "Taiwan, Inc. model." Both of these models assume that policy outcomes are the result of an evaluation of choices by a coherent elite with shared perceptions of the values to be maximized in response to perceived problems. The state is portrayed as a unitary, rational actor seeking to maximize its own interests, and a state action is considered to be a calculated response to a strategic problem.[1]

The rationality model and the Taiwan, Inc. model are both suitable for analyzing Taiwan's political economy in the 1950s and 1960s. During this takeoff period, the Taiwanese state had a strong political leadership and an economic policy apparatus staffed with reformist technocrats who operated through ad hoc cabinet boards and economic commissions.[2] One of these, the Industrial Development Commission (IDC) was responsible for planning Taiwan's industrial development strategies in the 1950s and early 1960s. Led by the ambitious K. Y. Yin, a client of Premier Chen Cheng, and other technocrats, this supraministerial commission intervened directly in the market and played a key role in promoting Taiwan's export-oriented growth. As Wang Chou-ming and K. T. Li (Li Kwoh-ting) later recalled, the IDC, staffed by forty-seven engineering specialists, was a highly efficient instrument. Decisions were made quickly, and proposals were implemented with impressive speed and without the cumbrous paperwork associated with the rest of the bureaucracy. Yin's competence and assertiveness enabled him to win the cooperation of other sectors of the state, and the IDC promoted two hundred projects within the space of two years and became the cradle of Taiwan's future economic elite.[3]

In their analysis of Taiwan's economic policymaking, scholars who adopt the rationality and Taiwan, Inc. models assume that, in this period, decisionmakers exhibited a high degree of harmony and cooperation under the leadership of a charismatic ruler. In this kind of political environment, technocrats remained insulated from political intervention and economic policies were postulated according to the principle of maximizing economic benefits. This was indeed the case in Taiwan in the 1950s and 1960s.

However, these models are not really applicable to the situation in Taiwan today. In analyzing Taiwan's cross-Straits economic policy in the postdemocratization era, it is hardly possible to presume the existence of a coherent policymaking body. After the "decompression" process and the dismantling of authoritarian rule, various factors, such as business interests, proindependence sentiment, and factional concerns make themselves felt in the making of Taiwan's China policy. Different sectors of the state have different perceptions of benefit maximization, and this leads to conflict and disharmony within the state apparatus.

An alternative model for analyzing policymaking is the bureaucratic politics model. Compared to the rationality model, this model sees not one unitary actor but many actors and focuses not on a single strategic issue but on many diverse intranational problems and personal as well as organizational goals. Hence, state policies are not made by rational choice but by the "pulling and hauling that is politics."[4] As Graham Allison correctly points out, an action performed by a nation is the outcome of bargaining among individuals and groups within the government. The bureaucratic politics model helps to reveal the "pulling and hauling" that yields the action in question.[5]

This chapter will use the bureaucratic politics model to analyze the conflicts and interagency bargaining involved in the making of Taiwan's economic policy toward China. Emphasis will be placed on relations within and among bureaucracies and the role of the bureaucracies in the policymaking process. The chapter will begin with a discussion of the structural distribution of resources and authority in the sphere of China policy. The key players in the policymaking process will then be identified and their interaction and consensus-building activities will be described. The last part of the chapter will comprise a discussion of the implications of the change in state capacity in Taiwan.

Institutional Framework of Taiwan's
China Policymaking

From a formal institutional perspective, Taiwan's China policy system may be divided into three levels: policymaking, policy coordination, and policy implementation. At the very top of the whole system is the National Unification Council, a task force headed by the president himself with the vice president and the premier as his deputies. The NUC consists of the heads of the five Yuans, or branches of the ROC government, the secretary-general of the National Assembly, representatives from political parties, high-ranking politicians, scholars, entrepreneurs, grassroots leaders, and labor representatives.[6] It functions as an advisory organ providing the president with guidance, suggestions, and research findings for use in formulating fundamental policies on national unification.

The Mainland Affairs Council under the Executive Yuan (cabinet) is a formal administrative agency under the supervision of the premier. It is in charge of researching, planning, deliberating, coordinating, and to some extent implementing Taiwan's China (or "mainland") policy and other related issues. It is also responsible to the Legislative Yuan, as stipulated in the ROC Constitution. Members of the Council itself include all ministers and related commission chairpersons.

The Straits Exchange Foundation is a quasi-nongovernmental organization handling matters of a technical nature arising in the course of people-to-people exchanges with the PRC. These matters touch upon the authority of the ROC government but cannot be handled by the government directly under current policy (see Figure 4.1).

In reality, the NUC has only symbolic functions. With twenty-eight members from a variety of backgrounds, it acts more as a channel of communication and a discussion group than as a decisionmaking body. However, it does perform two crucial functions. First, in response to the rising demand for participation from society as a whole and opposition forces in particular, the existence of the NUC gives the impression that China policy is the result of the integration of opinions from all sectors of society. Second, through the NUC, the state delivers a message to the general public in Taiwan and the government of the PRC that the ultimate goal of Taiwan's China policy is national unification, not separation. This helps to wrap policies such as "one country, two governments," "one country, two areas," and "one country, two political entities" in a cloak of "one China" orthodoxy.

According to the formal division of labor within the government, the formulation of China policy should be the responsibility of the Executive Yuan Council, headed by the premier and consisting of all ministers and

FIGURE 4.1   Organizational System of China Policy in Taiwan

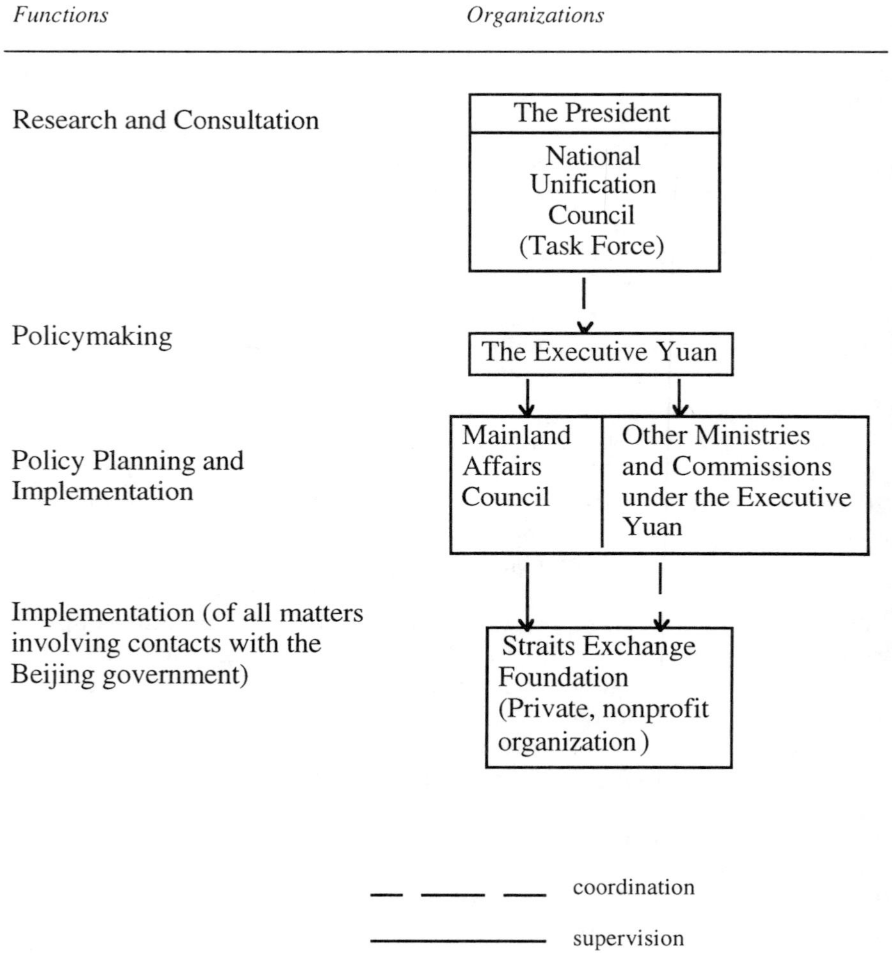

Functions   *Organizations*

Research and Consultation

```
┌─────────────────────────┐
│      The President       │
├─────────────────────────┤
│       National           │
│       Unification        │
│        Council           │
│      (Task Force)        │
└─────────────────────────┘
            │
            ▼
```

Policymaking

```
┌─────────────────────────┐
│    The Executive Yuan    │
└─────────────────────────┘
      │           │
      ▼           ▼
```

Policy Planning and
Implementation

```
┌──────────┬──────────────┐
│ Mainland │ Other Ministries │
│ Affairs  │ and Commissions  │
│ Council  │ under the Executive │
│          │ Yuan             │
└──────────┴──────────────┘
      │           │
```

Implementation (of all matters
involving contacts with the
Beijing government)

```
      ▼           ▼
┌─────────────────────────┐
│   Straits Exchange       │
│   Foundation             │
│   (Private, nonprofit    │
│   organization)          │
└─────────────────────────┘
```

— —— —   coordination

——————————   supervision

SOURCE: *Introduction to the Republic of China's Organization for the Handling of Mainland Affairs* (Taipei: Mainland Affairs Council, 1994).

ministers of state. But according to current practice, it is the president, in consultation with the premier, who decides the general orientation of the government's China policy. The council simply plays a consultative role and provides an arena in which policy is legitimized. The substantial policy-making functions of the Executive Yuan Council have been devolved to the MAC, which plays a key role in the formulation, planning, and implementation of China policy.

The MAC is on a level with other government ministries and councils, and its policymaking body, the Council consisting of the heads of ministries related to mainland affairs, meets once every two months. According to the MAC's Organic Regulations, the opinions of all the Council members (ministers) carry equal weight. It is the MAC's job to coordinate these different opinions and integrate them into the final policy proposal.[8]

One good example of how the MAC works can be found in the handling of the economic aspects of China policy. The MAC's Economic Affairs Department is divided into four functional sections, responsible for trade and investment, agriculture, financial affairs, and transportation. Through the Economic Affairs Task Group, which convenes once every two months, the MAC coordinates the policy-formulation work of other related ministries and bureaus.[9] Besides that, a monthly coordination meeting at vice ministerial level discusses more substantial issues concerning regulations and policies. Proposals of the coordination meeting are submitted to the Council for final decision.[10]

Parallel to the state institutional framework is the KMT's "mainland affairs" system (see Figures 4.2 and 4.3). The main purpose of the KMT's Mainland Affairs Guiding Group, established in 1988 and reorganized in 1991, is to integrate the formulation and implementation of the party's China policy. More important, the Guiding Group was established to ensure that the party would dominate state institutions in China policy formulation. According to Tseng Fu-wen, secretary-general of the KMT's Department of Mainland Operations, the Guiding Group's function is to "lead and guide" the general direction of the government's China policy. The main tasks of the Guiding Group are, first, the planning and discussion of China policy, and, second, the deliberation of resolutions made by the Central Standing Committee of the KMT and the party's chairman. Through a process of party-state coordination, the relevant state sectors implement decisions made by the Guiding Group.[11] From this point of view, the Guiding Group should be the real core decisionmaking body within the KMT hierarchy. However, contrary to what one might expect, the Guiding Group only convened twice during the eighteen months from July 1992 to January 1994, and its decisions were of little importance.[12]

FIGURE 4.2 Mainland Affairs System of KMT, 1992

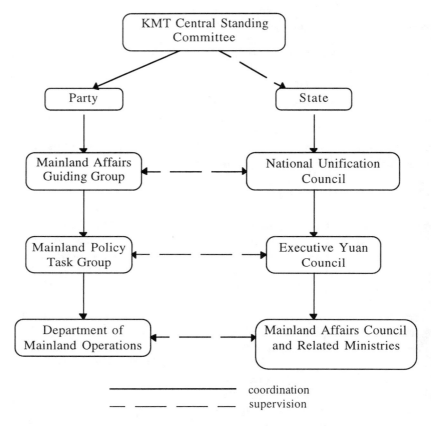

SOURCE: Adapted from *Lianhe bao* (United Daily News), July 20, 1993.

FIGURE 4.3   Adjusted Party and State Structure of Mainland Affairs
Policymaking, June 1993

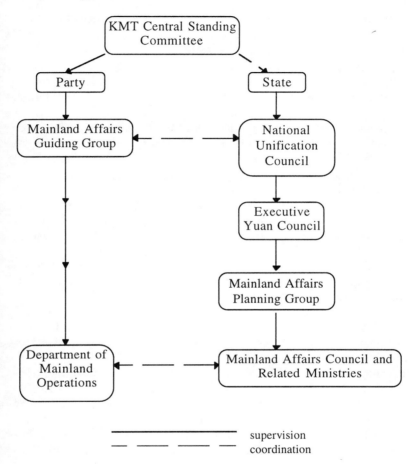

Until June 1993, the KMT had another body, the Mainland Policy Task Group, directly subordinate to the Guiding Group and on a level with the Executive Yuan Council in the state hierarchy. The Task Group was supposed to be responsible for policy implementation and party-state coordination, but because the Guiding Group was largely quiescent and the Task Group itself had very limited decisionmaking power, the latter had very little business to handle and convened infrequently.

The Department of Mainland Operations (DMO) of the KMT acted as the staff of the Task Group. During the Cold War era, the DMO, which was closely associated with the regime's security apparatus, was responsible for collecting and analyzing intelligence from China. Its importance has diminished since the lifting of martial law and the opening up of relations between Taiwan and China. The decline in importance of the DMO is reflected in the change in the status of its director-general. In the early 1990s, the DMO was headed by Alexander Cheng, a deputy secretary-general of the KMT and the son of Cheng Chieh-ming, a former head of the secret service. After the death of Alexander Cheng, the DMO was without a head for about two years before the appointment of its current director-general, Huang Yao-yu. Huang is a much less prominent member of the party hierarchy than his predecessor; his ranking in the KMT's Fourteenth Central Committee election was 148th, far behind all the leaders of the state mainland affairs bureaucracy.[13]

In June 1993, this parallel party-state policymaking system was reorganized. The KMT's Task Group was abolished and a new institution, the Mainland Affairs Planning Group, under the Executive Yuan, was established (see Figure 4.3).

The Planning Group is more selective and focused in terms of its members than either the Task Group or the Executive Yuan Council. Its twelve members include the vice premier, the presidential spokesman/deputy secretary-general of the Presidential Office, the chairman and one vice chairman of the MAC, the secretary-general of the SEF, and some other ministers.[14] This means that the Planning Group is small enough to include only the real China policymaking elite, yet big enough to include most relevant bodies. The Planning Group meets once a week—much more frequently than the KMT's Task Group. However, the new institution has attracted some criticism. People have argued that the functions of the Planning Group overlap with those of the Executive Yuan Council and the Mainland Affairs Council meeting. Moreover, the establishment of the Planning Group is not based on law but on executive order, so there are also doubts about its democratic accountability.

According to Kao Koong-lian, vice chairman of the MAC, the function of the Planning Group is to "handle immediate, unexpected, and important affairs. . . . The main function is consultation, not policymaking.

There is no overlap with the functions of the MAC, and there is no intention to replace the MAC."[15]

A closer examination of the operations of the Planning Group reveals it to be far more than a "consultative" body. Instead, it operates as a crisis management group and plays a role similar to the National Security Council in the United States. Headed by the vice premier, its decisions have a binding effect on subordinate ministries.

The Planning Group held its first meeting on July 9, 1993, when it set the agenda for the follow-up negotiations of the Koo-Wang talks, going so far as to designate the negotiators and fix the date and location of the first follow-up talks in Taipei.[16] During the Taipei talks in December that year, SEF negotiators had to report to the Planning Group every evening and wait for further instructions.[17] After a dispute arose in January 1994 between the MAC and the Ministry of Economic Affairs (MOEA) on the issue of direct transportation across the Straits, the Planning Group made the final decision, declaring that Minister P. K. Chiang's proposal for direct transportation reflected his "personal opinion," and that government policy would remain unchanged.[18]

In brief, through the establishment of the Planning Group, the state was trying to achieve closer coordination and integration among the mainland affairs bureaucracies. Before the establishment of the Planning Group, there had been fierce interagency conflicts between the MAC and both the SEF and the MOEA. Since the Planning Group convenes more frequently and its policymaking level is higher than that of the MAC, it was expected to play a decisive role in such interagency conflicts.

However, the MAC still plays a determining, although not an entirely dominant, role in the Planning Group. Its chairman and one vice chairman are both members, and the MAC is responsible for setting the Planning Group's agenda and performing backup staff work. Each member of the Planning Group has equal voting rights, but the MAC representatives constitute a "determining minority," and they can reverse decisions made by the majority. For instance, in July 1993 the MAC reversed a majority decision of the Planning Group to allow the SEF secretary-general Cheyne J. Y. Chiu to lead a fact-finding group to China and to discuss the agenda of the follow-up negotiations with his mainland counterparts. In response to opposition from the MAC, the Planning Group chairman Hsu Li-teh adopted a compromise solution: The SEF could decide who should lead the fact-finding group, but its mission should be limited to economic issues only.[19] On the direct cross-Straits transportation issue mentioned above, the MOEA declined to submit its proposal to the Planning Group because P. K. Chiang knew that it would be blocked by the MAC. Instead, Chiang chose to resort to the mass media to express his discontent.[20]

In conclusion, even after the establishment of the supraministerial Planning Group, the dominant player in the mainland affairs bureaucracy is still the MAC. The state will no doubt add new sectors to the bureaucracy in the future as the demand for coordination increases, and the MAC will try to grasp even more power. Also, as the influence of the party's mainland affairs bureaucracy diminishes, the MAC's predominance is becoming even more obvious. Moreover, the inclusion in the Planning Group of the deputy secretary-general of the Presidential Office, a figure outside the formal executive system, symbolizes the president's leading role in the Group. From this perspective, the Planning Group is an institution for ensuring that Lee Teng-hui's policy is implemented through the MAC.

The Straits Exchange Foundation and Institutional Conflicts

At the present stage, contacts between Taiwan and China are conducted through nongovernmental agencies. The state bureaucracies are responsible for policy planning and implementation, but technical matters that arise in the course of people-to-people interaction and that require contacts with Chinese officials are handled through the Straits Exchange Foundation, a nonofficial corporate body established in 1990. According to the "Guidelines for National Unification," the establishment of official channels of communication will have to wait until the "medium-term stage" of relations between the two sides, which can only be entered into after a certain degree of mutual trust and cooperation has been built up.[21]

The original idea was that the SEF's relationship with the MAC should be the same as that between the Ministry of Foreign Affairs (MOFA) and the Taipei Economic and Cultural Representative Office (TECRO) in Washington. TECRO, though an "unofficial" body, has acted as Taiwan's embassy in the United States since the termination of diplomatic relations in 1979, receiving direct instructions from the MOFA. In effect, TECRO is a semiofficial subordinate of the MOFA.

However, the situation between the MAC and the SEF is different. Whereas TECRO may be regarded as a branch of the government, the SEF is a corporate body. Although the SEF receives almost 80 percent of its funding from the state, its highest policymaking body is the Board of Trustees, on which the state occupies nine of the forty-nine seats.[22] Whereas TECRO's goal is to appear as "official" as possible and to undertake more "political" tasks, the SEF is supposed to remain "unofficial" and avoid "political contacts" with its Chinese counterparts. Restricted by this special political concern, the SEF finds it difficult to perform its tasks efficiently. The SEF's ambiguous status as both an "official" and an "unof-

TABLE 4.1   Directors of MAC and SEF, 1990–1993

Name	*Huang Kun-huei*	*Chen Charng-ven*	*Chen Rong-jye*	*Cheyne J.Y. Chiu*
Title	Chairman of MAC	Secretary-General of SEF	Secretary-General of SEF	Secretary-General of SEF
Tenure	05/91–10/94	11/90–03/92	03/92–03/93	03/93–10/93
Date of Birth	1936	1944	1943	1936
Place of Birth	Taiwan	Fujian	Taiwan	Jiangsu
Academic Background	Ed.D., University of Northern Colorado	S.J.D., Harvard University	S.J.D., Southern Methodist University	LL.B., National Chengchi University
Career Background	Professor; Director, Youth Dept. of KMT; Minister of State	Partner, Lee & Li Attorneys-at-Law; Consultant, Ministry of National Defense	Director, Dept. of Treaty & Legal Aff., MOFA	Ambassador; Deputy Secretary-General of Presidential Office

SOURCE: *The Republic of China Yearbook 1993* (Taipei: Government Information Office, 1993).

ficial" body leads to confusion over how autonomous it should be or how far it should subordinate itself to the state bureaucracy.

The relationship between the MAC and the SEF is far from harmonious. After several direct confrontations, the length of tenure of the SEF's secretary-general decreased from nineteen months to thirteen months, then to nine months.[23] The *hailu dazhan*—"battle between the sea [the SEF] and the land [the MAC]"—often hits the headlines in the Taiwan press (see Table 4.1).

As a member of Taiwan's biggest law firm and a prominent opinion leader, the SEF's first secretary-general, Chen Charng-ven, made a big career sacrifice when he devoted himself to cross-Straits relations in 1990. However, his arrogance toward politicians, especially legislators, was considered to be a major reason for his forced resignation less than two years later. Chen was particularly defiant toward the Legislative Yuan, refusing to be interpellated by a meeting of its budget and finance committees on the grounds that, as a nonofficial body, the SEF should not be subject to legislative oversight. His stubborn gesture on this occasion resulted in a direct verbal confrontation with legislators. Finally, in June 1991 the Legislative Yuan passed a resolution requesting that the secretary-general of the SEF be a full-time position, forcing Chen to choose between the SEF and his legal career. In February 1992, Chen decided to resign.[24]

Chen's own attitude was just one of several reasons for his being forced out, however. Factional politics was a more important factor. As a long-term legal consultant for the Ministry of National Defense, Chen had developed a close relationship with Hau Pei-tsun when Hau was chief of the general staff in the 1980s. After the KMT split into mainstream and nonmainstream factions in early 1990, Chen was classified as belonging to Hau's nonmainstream group. During Hau's premiership from May 1990, mainstream legislators were in the majority in the Legislative Yuan, and therefore confrontations with Chen Charng-ven became part of the "proxy war" between the two competing factions. Most resolutions urging Chen to resign were proposed by legislators from the DPP and from pro–Lee Teng-hui groupings in the KMT, such as the Wisdom Coalition and the Concord Association.

Moreover, there was an ethnic element in this antipathy to Chen. As an "arrogant mainlander," Chen's efforts to promote cross-Straits interaction aroused suspicions of a "rush toward unification" or a "betrayal of the Taiwanese people." These suspicions may be discerned in the wording of interpellations and motions submitted by DPP legislators who preferred to see a slowdown in Taiwan-China interaction.[25] This ethnic factor further blocked any positive action by Chen's SEF to create normal channels of communication with China.

Chen Charng-ven's successor, Chen Rong-jye, was a Taiwan-born career diplomat. His Taiwanese background spared him from becoming embroiled in the "unification-independence" controversy and from accusations of "betraying Taiwan," but his tenure was cut short by a clash of personalities and institutional conflicts.

According to the Organic Law of the Straits Exchange Foundation, the SEF's business is divided into "independent" and "authorized" categories.[26] With regard to its "independent" business, the SEF considers that since it is not a branch of the government, it should enjoy autonomy in handling ordinary and "nonofficial" matters unconnected with those that it is authorized to handle by the government. It was in this spirit that the SEF established its Travel Services and Cultural Services departments.[27] More important, most staff members of the SEF come from the private sector, and they are accustomed to a flexible and efficient style of management very different from that of the civil service. These people are eager to undertake the task of breaking the ice in relations between Taiwan and China.

However, the MAC has a different opinion of the status of the SEF. In March 1992 it promulgated an executive order, the Principles Governing the Handling of MAC-SEF Relations (known as the "nine points") without consulting the SEF. In these nine points, the MAC defined the SEF as "a corporate body in the eyes of the general public, but actually a semi-executive institution representing the state." Appointments to all top posts in the SEF, including the secretary-general, the deputy secretaries-general, and the department heads had to be approved by the MAC, visits to China by SEF personnel required the prior consent of the MAC, and the SEF had to obey current state policies and regulations and could operate only within the sphere of governmental authorization.[28] This was very different from how the SEF envisaged itself, and conflict seemed to be inevitable.

The first conflicts broke out in March 1992, one month after Chen Rongjye was appointed secretary-general. Chen had been instructed to discuss the issue of document verification during his first trip to China, but once he arrived in Xiamen, he opened a new round of negotiations with his mainland counterpart on the subject of inviting Chinese journalists to visit Taiwan. When the MAC criticized the SEF for "exceeding its sphere of authorization," the SEF argued that inviting journalists was part of its "independent business," which did not require the MAC's authorization.[29]

For the same reason, when the SEF Board of Trustees passed a resolution to support "Project Hope" in China,[30] the MAC objected, claiming that Project Hope was merely a scheme for enticing Taiwan into political contacts with China and that any decisions related to politics should be taken by the MAC.[31] More serious conflicts broke out over Chen Rongjye's trip to Xiamen in September 1992, when Chen gave the MAC only oral notification of his departure. The MAC considered that because the SEF was a subordinate organization, a formal written notification was necessary. In addition, during this visit, Chen met with his mainland counterpart, Zou Zhekai, without the consent of the MAC.[32]

As a result of these two organizations' different perceptions of the SEF's tasks and status, conflicts between them escalated. Finally, a direct confrontation occurred between Chen and the MAC chairman Huang Kunhuei, when they were appearing before a joint meeting of the legal and internal affairs committees of the Legislative Yuan in January 1993. When Chen complained that he was "confined to a wheelchair," Huang retorted by emphasizing the "political nature" of mainland affairs, and said that the SEF should be able to do a good job even though it was "in a wheelchair."[33] The result of this emotional confrontation was the resignation of Chen in March that year.

The state's capacity in China policymaking was badly damaged by these clashes between the SEF and the MAC. The public was also demanding structural and personnel changes. When President Lee Tenghui appointed his close associate, presidential spokesman Cheyne Chiu, as secretary-general of the SEF in March 1993, it was generally assumed that this would mark the beginning of a more cooperative relationship between the SEF and the MAC. However, Chiu's first job as secretary-general—the Koo-Wang talks in April—was actually the start of a new round of conflicts. Both the preliminary arrangements and the agenda for the actual negotiations were strictly overseen and checked by the MAC. The SEF had very limited autonomy at the negotiating table, while ARATS, its Chinese counterpart, was fully authorized by the PRC's State Council. Chiu's frustration in Singapore threw a shadow over future cooperation between the MAC and the SEF.

The following months were marked by an escalation of conflict. Chiu insisted on autonomy in the appointment of personnel within the SEF, and he promoted H. Y. Hsu to the post of deputy secretary-general without the MAC's approval. His request to increase the number of SEF negotiators was rejected, and in June 1993 conflict broke out again over the visit of deputy secretary-general Lee Ching-ping to China. Finally, a complete break occurred at an SEF press conference on June 18, when Cheyne Chiu said:

> The attitude of the MAC is purely that of the *yamen* [government office in imperial China]. . . . The Principles Governing the Handling of MAC-SEF Relations is an "unequal treaty" per se. In my opinion, our relationship with the MAC should be that of brothers, not father and son. However, in the Koo-Wang talks, the MAC even specified the color of our ties, the style of our suits. The MAC only assigns very low-level officials to attend the SEF-MAC coordination meetings. All this implies disdain for the SEF. . . . In this situation, either Huang Kun-huei resigns, or I leave.[34]

The conflict between the SEF and the MAC this time was more a personal clash between Chiu and Huang. Both were close clients of Lee Teng-hui, but Huang, a native Taiwanese, joined Lee's camp much earlier, having served under the president when he was mayor of Taipei and governor of Taiwan province.[35] Chiu, by contrast, had been a diplomat for more than twenty years, and his access to Lee dated only from his appointment as deputy secretary-general to the president in the late 1980s, and later presidential spokesman. In this case, the degree of access to the highest officeholder determined the resources each player could command in the political game. Huang's long history of access to Lee and his status as a native Taiwanese gave him the power to resist three capable secretaries-general of the SEF.

There was also a difference in personal style between Huang and Chiu. As one of Huang's subordinates at the MAC has noted, Huang, "over-emphasizes external public relations, personal status, access, and hierarchy. His administrative style is that of a hegemon. The policymaking process is not a consensus-building process, but one of top-down direct orders."[36]

By contrast, Chiu had a more progressive view of cross-Straits relations. During his tenure as presidential spokesman and executive secretary of the National Unification Council, he suggested tripartite talks involving Taiwan, China, and Hong Kong to discuss the "Guidelines for National Unification," and in 1992 he proposed that Taiwan and China should sign a mutual nonaggression treaty.[37] However, as the SEF secretary-general, Chiu was in a difficult position—for instance, he had to obey the orders of his former subordinates in the NUC (in the bureaucratic hierarchy, the NUC executive secretary ranks much higher than even the chairman of the MAC)—and his image as the "president's man" failed to get him anywhere in the mainland affairs bureaucracy. Finally, he demonstrated his discontent at the KMT's Fourteenth Congress in August 1993 by standing for election to the Central Committee. Chiu's activism earned him thirty-seventh place in the list of successful candidates, much higher than Huang Kun-huei, who ranked fifty-seventh.[38] At the end of the year, Chiu submitted his resignation for the third time, and it was accepted.

In conclusion, the SEF-MAC confrontation provides a good illustration of the changing nature of the Taiwanese state. First, we can see how democratization has led to a split in the political elite, and how the patron-client relationship has become much more important in political appointments in general and in the mainland affairs bureaucracy in particular. The degree of access to President Lee Teng-hui determines an official's real power. That is why Huang Kun-huei was able to survive three SEF secretaries-general.

Second, ethnicity and ideological factors have emerged as the crucial elements in Taiwanese politics. The main task at the highest policymaking level is to balance different factional forces and ethnicity. For instance, it is assumed that since both Huang Kun-huei and the chairman of the SEF, Koo Chen-fu, are native Taiwanese, the secretary-general of the SEF and at least one of the MAC vice chairpersons must be a mainlander. This ethnic factor is always associated with the unification-independence tangle in Taiwanese society. Hence, the activism of Chen Charng-ven and Cheyne Chiu was interpreted as promoting rapid unification. Their actions were then opposed by the DPP and proindependence forces within the KMT. Under these internal and external pressures, the MAC has had to play the role of the brake in relations with China. This may explain why, after the breakthrough of the Koo-Wang talks, the MAC seemed to cool down and to deter Cheyne Chiu from taking further action. From this perspective, the MAC-SEF standoff is an indirect outcome of political contradictions in society.

Third, it is clear that the true manipulator of China policy is President Lee Teng-hui himself. The tussle between Chen Charng-ven and Huang Kun-huei was seen as a "proxy war" between Lee's mainstream faction and Hau Pei-tsun's nonmainstream faction, while Cheyne Chiu's appointment as the SEF secretary-general signified an intensified effort on

Lee's part to dominate China policy. However, after conflicts broke out between the two Lee clients, the president indicated by his silence that the institutionally superior party—the MAC—should win. The only way to ensure harmonious institutional interaction was to recognize that the "Huang Kun-huei line," and thus the "Lee Teng-hui line," was dominant.

Institutional Conflicts—The MAC Versus the Economic Bureaucracy

In formal terms, the Ministry of Economic Affairs is the state sector responsible for economic relations with China. However, as the preceding analysis shows, the MAC plays a dominant role in all aspects of China policymaking. Despite this overlap in responsibility, the two bodies hold different, sometimes opposite, views on cross-Straits economic ties.

P. K. Chiang, the minister of economic affairs, is a Taiwan-born, Tokyo University–educated specialist in Agricultural Economics. Before he became minister, Chiang's career had spanned diplomacy and international trade, and his posts had included those of director of the Board of Foreign Trade and political vice minister of economic affairs.[39] He has never shown any sign of factional affiliation, and his promotions were based primarily on professional expertise rather than on access to the highest political leader. Chiang's differences with the MAC chairman Huang Kun-huei may be characterized as a clash between a technocrat and a politician. Chiang also demonstrated a more progressive attitude to booming cross-Straits interaction, while Huang's style was conservative and bureaucratic.

Chiang's cross-Straits economic policy is more probusiness. First, he argues that investing in China will not weaken Taiwan's international competitiveness because most of the industries that are transferring their operations have already lost competitiveness anyway. By letting "sunset" industries move out, he insists, and switching to production of high value-added products, Taiwan can upgrade its industrial sector and promote a division of labor between Taiwan and China. Second, his response to those who argue that China could wreck Taiwan's economy by suddenly cutting off economic ties is to point out that this would hurt China more than it would hurt Taiwan, because China's imports from across the Straits consist mostly of industrial raw materials, machine tools, and capital, all of which are vital to China's manufacturing industries. Third, Chiang denies that Taiwanese businessmen in China could become "political hostages"; these businesses are still based outside China, and they could easily adjust to changing circumstances, he argues. Finally, Chiang is convinced that state policies should abide by the rules of the market.

Businesspeople are profit seeking, and it is impossible to change their behavior by means of administrative orders.[40]

The MAC, on the other hand, emphasizes the political side of doing business with China. In a special relationship of this kind, the MAC believes, political considerations should take precedence over economics and the market mechanism. As Huang Kun-huei said, economic benefits are not the only consideration in formulating economic policy toward China. More important issues are politics, legal issues, and national security, and among these politics should always be given first priority. From the MAC's perspective, as Taiwan becomes more economically dependent on China, the political risks will increase. The PRC's policy is to link trade relations to its united front campaign against Taiwan, and its ultimate goal is to use business ties to effect a change in Taiwan's policy. All in all, China policy, including its economic aspects, must be implemented according to the "Guidelines for National Unification." To use Huang's own words, the MAC should have the final say in any interinstitutional conflict.[41]

To sum up, both the MAC and the MOEA recognize that economic relations with China have played an important part in Taiwan's economic development. But while the MAC's stance is to keep the Taiwan economy insulated from Chinese political influence, the MOEA is eager to grasp this historic opportunity to boost Taiwan's economic development. Opportunity knocks only once. If Taiwan does not act now, the MOEA believes, advanced countries such as the United States and Japan, or Taiwan's economic rivals, such as South Korea, will go ahead and take it. These different perceptions of cross-Straits economic relations have led to inevitable conflicts between the MAC and the MOEA.

After the Koo-Wang talks in April 1993, the prospects looked good for better relations between Taiwan and China. However, subsequent developments soon destroyed this optimistic atmosphere. The Koo-Wang talks helped Taiwan develop an image as an equal political entity to the PRC, and it was after this historic encounter that Taipei launched its propaganda campaign aimed at Taiwan returning to the United Nations, which won support among the Latin American countries. Then, in August that year, the PRC released its white paper on the Taiwan question in which it reiterated its stance that Taiwan is just a renegade local government without any legal international status.[42] This started a new round of confrontation between Taiwan and China and caused the December 1993 follow-up talks in Taipei to end in stalemate.

In this atmosphere of gloom, P. K. Chiang tried to go against the stream and seek a new breakthrough in cross-Straits trade. During a press conference in November 1993, Chiang announced that the government's policy toward cross-Straits trade and investment would change from one of discouragement and noninterference to one of positive guidance. The MOEA would also scrap its list of permitted areas of investment and replace it with a list of those areas in which Taiwanese businesses were prohibited from investing.[43] This astonishing policy shift was welcomed by business circles and the general public.[44]

However, on the following day the MAC vice chairman Kao Koong-lian and the political vice minister of economic affairs, Yang Shih-chien, held an extraordinary joint press conference during which they asserted that Chiang had only been expressing his personal opinion. Kao argued that changes in investment policy are related to Taiwan's overall economic situation, the division of labor, and other issues crucial to Taiwan's existence. Such changes could not be decided by the MOEA alone.[45] Kao's words signified the MAC's rejection of Chiang's liberalization proposal.

This was by no means an isolated incident. It reflected a lack of coordination and insufficient channels of formal communication within the state bureaucracy. The Mainland Affairs Planning Group, which was added to the state hierarchy specifically for this purpose, was obviously not doing its job. Dissident opinions should have been discussed and resolved before, not after, the policy was made public. Yet if the state hierarchy does not provide a forum in which all opinions are listened to without prejudice, the only way ministers can relieve their discontent is by going public. On the other hand, Chiang's announcement may have had other political implications. He could have been using it as a trial balloon to test the reaction of society at large, especially the business sector. As a liberal-minded economic bureaucrat, he may have thought he could increase his bargaining power by forging an alliance with private business to push for the reform of state policies.

The discontent in the MOEA is not limited to the minister himself. It can be seen in the statements of other key economic bureaucrats and in the ministry's concrete actions. After a fact-finding visit to China in November 1993, the chairman of the MOEA's Investment Commission, Chen Ming-bang, urged that politics and economics be kept separate and requested a large-scale opening up of investment to boost cross-Straits trade. Without hesitation, the MAC responded that Chen was acting irresponsibly and that he had been misguided by Chinese propaganda.[46]

The MAC has even intervened at the administrative level, in decisions concerning investment in China. In January 1993, the MOEA was preparing to add seventy-four items to the list of permitted investments, but when the MAC objected to two out of the seventy-four, the whole proposal was blocked.[47] The MAC even issued an official request to the MOEA that it should in the future submit a draft of any such proposal before it was announced.[48]

It seemed that the MAC had become superior to the MOEA, and that it was a kind of superministry. However, according to Kao Koong-lian, the formal process of policymaking was as follows: "The general principles and regulations of cross-Straits economic relations are discussed in the MAC. Once the principle is confirmed, the MOEA is responsible for implementation. For instance, the MAC decides the principle governing the importation of goods from the mainland, and the MOEA decides what items can be imported. The process is the same for indirect investments in the mainland."[49]

It is obvious that the MAC's actions in this respect are arbitrary and a deviation from the original institutional design. Although the deputy director of the MAC's Department of Economic Affairs, Tseng Chen-hsiung, has repeated that the MAC plays only a coordinating role,[50] the case of the investment list mentioned above indicates that the confusion and contradictions in Taiwan's economic policy toward China results largely from the MAC's authoritarian attitudes and actions. The MAC not only postulates general and abstract principles but also interferes in the routine work of the economic bureaucracy. This creates the strange situation of the "amateur" leading the "professional," and politics leading the economy. Even in the authoritarian era of the 1950s and 1960s, direct political interference in economic affairs was rare.

Another interagency conflict occurred over the issue of direct transportation. The ban on direct contacts with China means that ships and aircraft must transit through Hong Kong or another third country. This increases the cost of cross-Straits trade and causes a great deal of inconvenience.

At the end of 1993, P. K. Chiang told the press that the MOEA would find a way to permit direct transportation between designated points without contravening the "Guidelines for National Unification." He suggested that transportation agreements be concluded on a city-to-city basis, thus avoiding the sovereignty issue.[51] This proposal also won the support of the Ministry of Transportation and Communications (MOTC).

The MAC, however, took the opposite view. Huang Kun-huei argued that on the issue of direct transportation, politics should take precedence over economics. The MAC even released a formal public explanation of its policy in an effort to resist pressure from other government agencies and from society. From the 1994 revised edition of the "Problems and Prospect of Cross-Straits Direct Transportation," it is clear that the MAC's objections were one-sided rather than being based on cost-benefit analysis. The document listed three main categories of obstacles preventing the opening of direct transportation: (1) *political obstacles*—China must end its hostility toward Taiwan, recognize Taiwan as an equal political entity, and stop blocking Taiwan's participation in the international community before direct links can be permitted; (2) *legal obstacles*—the parties to official transportation agreements must recognize one another's political legitimacy, which involves the issue of sovereignty; (3) *security obstacles*—while China remains hostile to Taiwan, the opening of direct transportation links can only damage Taiwan's air and naval security.[52]

The MAC even rejected all "expedient solutions" to the direct transportation issue, including those proposed by the MOEA. From the MAC's perspective, the difference between these variant proposals and normal direct transportation was quantitative rather than qualitative. From an economic point of view, whereas the MOEA wanted to promote trade through direct transportation, the MAC argued that direct transportation—and hence direct trade—would increase Taiwan's economic dependence on China and make it more vulnerable to political pressure from Beijing.

To sum up, the controversy about direct transportation reflects a conflict between two approaches to policymaking: panpoliticization and cost-benefit analysis. The MOEA and the MOTC put economic considerations first and are willing to adopt a more flexible approach to such problems as flag carrying and national defense. The MAC gives priority to security and national dignity and is willing to sacrifice economic benefits in order to keep to the "Guidelines for National Unification."

The issue revealed a serious lack of coordination between the different sectors of the bureaucracy. The MOEA announced its policy without discussing it with the MAC, then the MAC countered with the release of a formal policy explanation before resorting to the Mainland Affairs Guiding Group, where P. K. Chiang's proposals were labeled an "individual opinion." These conflicts often encourage dissidents within the bureaucracy to resort to the mass media. For instance, after Chiang's direct-transportation proposal was rejected in January 1994, he told the press, to everyone's surprise, that 60 percent of goods bound for Hong Kong from Taiwan were actually exported directly to China, far more than the MAC's estimate of 20 percent.[53] Furthermore, he continued to argue that direct transportation is a good way of encouraging Taiwanese businesses to keep their roots in Taiwan.[5454]

Conclusion

In this chapter, we have discussed the structure of Taiwan's China policy bureaucracy, the distribution of power among its various branches, and the "pulling and hauling" that goes on in the formulation of Taiwan's economic policy toward China. Our analysis has revealed bureaucratic infighting, structural disorder, and confusion between political and economic goals within the state hierarchy.

From the macro perspective, institutional conflicts are a reflection of contradictions in Taiwan's political and social system. Factional politics were involved in the fall of SEF secretary-general Chen Charng-ven; ethnic factors not only block positive initiatives promoted by mainlander members of the political elite but also influence the distribution of power and bureaucratic appointments. Combined with the increase in independence sentiment inside and outside the state bureaucracy, these three factors—ethnicity, factional politics, and national identity—have become active components in the making of Taiwan's China policy. In these circumstances, it is no wonder that this policy is criticized for being conservative and lagging behind actual cross-Straits economic interaction.

It is interesting to note that this policymaking style is quite different from that of the 1950s and 1960s. In the authoritarian era, technocrats were largely free from political interference. Political conflicts and repression within the bureaucracy were not unknown, but they were limited to the higher levels. Economic bureaucrats could formulate policies according to actual economic demands in an environment insulated from political concerns. The supreme leader, Chiang Kai-shek, was well aware of his limitations in the economic sphere, and he allowed his close associate Chen Cheng and a group of technocrats to take responsibility for devising Taiwan's economic development strategies. Although Chiang was indeed an authoritarian leader, his openness in economic affairs was one of the determining factors in Taiwan's economic success in the 1960s.

By contrast, China policy in the 1990s has been in the hands of politicians and a nonprofessional elite. The MAC's longest serving chairman, Huang Kun-huei, earned his position not because of his expertise in economics or Chinese affairs but because of his access to President Lee Teng-hui. It was this advantage that allowed Huang to survive three secretaries-general of the SEF who were either legal experts or former diplomats and to resist an economics minister who had accumulated over twenty years' experience in handling economic affairs. In contrast to P. K. Chiang's more laissez-faire attitude to economic policymaking, Lee Teng-hui has tried to exert firm control over China policy through his protégé Huang Kun-huei.

From the preceding analysis, we can also discern a decline in the role of the KMT in the China policymaking process. The KMT's Mainland Affairs Guiding Group has almost ceased to function, its Mainland Policy Task Group was abolished in 1993, and the Department of Mainland Operations also plays a very marginal role in policymaking. In 1992, Lee Teng-hui initiated a "decisionmaking meeting" to take over the policymaking function of the KMT Central Standing Committee. The five permanent participants of this meeting are Lee himself, Vice President Li Yuan-zu, the premier, the secretary-general of the KMT, and the secretary-general of the Presidential Office. In addition, Lee may invite ministers to join the conference in their capacity as members of the KMT, but the conference is held in the Presidential Office.[55] This seems to imply a reconvergence of the party and the state in policymaking. In particular, real policymaking power is concentrated in the hands of the KMT chairman and state president.

In conclusion, the most powerful political resource of the dominant player in the formulation of Taiwan's China policy—the MAC—is the backing of the president. In these circumstances, dissident sectors of the state have to utilize resources outside the bureaucracy, such as the mass media and business interests, to boost their bargaining power. Hence, there has been much "pulling and hauling" between the MAC and the economic bureaucracy, and between political concerns and the demands of the market.

Notes

1. For the rationality model of policymaking, see Graham T. Allison, *Essence of Decision: Explaining the Cuban Missile Crisis* (Boston: Little Brown, 1971), chapter 1; Kenneth Lieberthal and Michael Oksenberg, *Policy Making in China* (Princeton: Princeton University Press, 1988), 11–15. The "Taiwan, Inc." model is adapted from Daniel Okimoto's "Japan, Inc." model. See Daniel I. Okimoto, "Political Inclusivity: The Domestic Structure of Trade," in vol. 1 of *The Political Economy of Japan*, ed. Takashi Inoguchi and Daniel I. Okimoto (Stanford: Stanford University Press, 1988), 306–307.

2. Stephan Haggard, *Pathways from the Periphery* (Ithaca: Cornell University Press, 1991), 87.

3. Kang Lu-tao, *Li Guoding koushu lishi* (An Oral History of Li Kwoh-ting) (Taipei: Chuo-yueh, 1993), chapter 5; Wang Chou-ming, "The Industrial Development Commission and Me," *Yuanjian* (The Global View), October 1993, 76–80. Wang Chou-ming joined Taiwan's Industrial Development Commission in 1953 and later served in the Ministry of Economic Affairs and the Ministry of Finance for about thirty years. K. T. Li was one of the main architects of Taiwan's industrial development. After earning an advanced degree in physics from Cambridge University, Li served as Minister of Economic Affairs and Minister of Finance from 1965 to 1976. In the 1950s and early 1960s he was a member of the Industrial Development Commission and secretary-general of the Commission for U.S. Aid. For further details of these two men, see *The Republic of China Yearbook 1993* (Taipei: Government Information Office, 1993), 653, 601.

4. Graham T. Allison, "Conceptual Models and the Cuban Missile Crisis," in *American Foreign Policy: Theoretical Essays*, ed. G. John Ikenberry (Glenview, Ill., Scott, Foresman and Company, 1989), 358.

5. Ibid., p. 362.

6. *Zhongguo shibao* (China Times) (Taipei), February 29, 1992.

7. *Introduction to the Republic of China's Organization for the Handling of Mainland Affairs* (Taipei: Mainland Affairs Council, 1994).

8. "Organic Regulations of the Mainland Affairs Council," in *Dalu gongzuo fagui huibian* (Collection of Regulations on Mainland Affairs Work) (Taipei: Mainland Affairs Council, 1993), 1–26.

9. Huang Kun-huei, "Report of the Mainland Affairs Council to the Legislative Yuan," (unpublished handout, Mainland Affairs Council, Taiwan, October 1993), 15.

10. *Lianhe bao* (United Daily News) (Taipei), August 13, 1993.

11. Tseng Fu-wen, secretary-general of the KMT's Department of Mainland Operations, Taipei, interview with the author, August 23, 1994.

12. Calculated from *Zili zaobao* (Independence Morning Post) (Taipei), July 29, 1993, and *Zhongguo shibao*, January 4, 1994.

13. Huang Kuang-chin, "Analysis of the KMT's Fourteenth Central Committee Election," *Xin xinwen* (The Journalist), August 28, 1993, 33.

14. *Zhongguo shibao*, July 3, 1993.

15. Speech at the MAC Council meeting, *Zhongguo shibao*, July 3, 1993.

16. *Zhongyang ribao* (Central Daily News), July 10, 1993.

17. *Zili zaobao*, December 9, 1994.

18. *Jingji ribao* (Economic Daily News), January 14, 1994.

19. *Zhongshi wanbao* (China Times Express), July 22, 1993.

20. *Jingji ribao*, January 14, 1994.

21. *Guojia tongyi gangling* (Guidelines for National Unification) (Taipei: Government Information Office, 1991).

22. *Caituan faren haixia jiaoliu jijinhui 82/83 nian nianbao* (Annual Report of Straits Exchange Foundation 1993) (Taipei: Straits Exchange Foundation, 1994), 27–29.

23. *Lianhe bao*, October 15, 1993.

24. *Zhongguo shibao*, July 21, 1991.

25. For the full text of the DPP's motions and interpellation, see *Ziyou shibao* (Liberty Times), December 15, 1991 and February 15, 1992.

26. Clause 3 of the "Organic Regulations of the Straits Exchange Foundation," in *Liang'an guanxi yu dalu zhengce* (Cross-Straits Relations and Mainland Policy), ed. Huang Tien-chung (Taipei: Wu-nan, 1993), appendix 3.

27. *Lianhe bao*, January 11, 1993.

28. "Principles Governing the Handling of MAC-SEF Relations," in *Haixia liang'an tongyi zhengcezhi yanjiu* (On the Unification Policies of the Two Sides of the Taiwan Straits), ed. Chu Hsin-min and Hung Chung-min (Taipei: Jung-jen, 1993), appendix 18.

29. *Lianhe bao*, January 21, 1992.

30. Project Hope is a scheme initiated by the Beijing government to attract private donations at home and overseas to support elementary education in remote areas of China.

31. *Lianhe bao*, January 21, 1992.

32. Ibid.

33. *Xin xinwen*, January 10, 1993, 66–68.

34. *Zhongguo shibao*, June 18, 1993.

35. Xu Ze, *Li Denghui pingzhuan* (A Critical Biography of Lee Teng-hui) (Hong Kong: Hsuan-huang, 1988), 54–55.

36. For the full text of this open letter from Kung Peng-cheng, the former director of the MAC's Cultural Affairs Department, see *Xin xinwen*, August 24, 1993, 38–39. Kung resigned in 1993 after a serious conflict with Huang.

37. *Xin xinwen*, March 13, 1993, 24.

38. Ibid., September 18, 1993, 17.

39. *The Republic of China Yearbook 1993*, 550.

40. Wu Ke, "Special Interview with Minister P. K. Chiang and Chairman Huang Kun-huei," *Shibao zhoukan* (China Times Weekly), January 12, 1994, 10–22; Liang Chung-wei, "Interview with P. K. Chiang," *Tianxia zazhi* (Commonwealth Magazine), March 1994, 65–84.

41. Wu, "Special Interview with Minister P. K. Chiang," 14.

42. Taiwan Affairs Office, PRC State Council, "The Taiwan Question and Reunification of China," *Beijing Review*, September 6–12, 1993, i–viii. For a detailed discussion of the PRC's white paper, see Chapter 3.

43. The former system implied that investment in China was prohibited in principle, whereas the publication of a list of areas in which Taiwanese were prohibited from investing gave the impression that investment was prohibited only in exceptional cases. This will be discussed in more detail in chapter 6.

44. *Lianhe bao*, November 11, 1993.

45. Ibid.

46. *Zili zaobao*, November 14, 1993.

47. *Gongshang shibao* (Commercial Times), January 22, 1993.

48. This was Document No. 100 of the MAC's Department of Economic Affairs. The original text reads: "Concerning the process of adding items of indirect investment and technical cooperation with the mainland, the Investment Commission of the MOEA shall collect all the data, and then submit it to the MAC. The final announcement may be made only after the MAC has carried out its review." See ibid.

49. Kao Koong-lian, *Liang'an jingmao xiankuang yu zhanwang* (Current Status and Prospects of Cross-Straits Economic Relations) (Taipei: Mainland Affairs Council, 1993), 6. Kao is a scholar turned bureaucrat who is responsible for economic affairs in the MAC.

50. Tseng Chen-hsiung, interview with the author, August 10, 1994.

51. *Lianhe bao*, December 30, 1993.

52. *Liang'an zhihangde wenti yu zhanwang* (Problems and Prospect of Cross-Straits Direct Transportation) (Taipei: Mainland Affairs Council, 1994), 1–18.

53. *Lianhe bao*, January 26, 1994.

54. Ibid., January 25, 1994.

55. Tsou Tu-chi, "Party-State Relations in Taiwan" (Ph.D. diss., National Chengchi University, 1993), 223.

5

State-Business Relations and Taiwan's Cross-Straits Economic Policy

In an analysis of Taiwan's political economy, the state-centered approach stresses the autonomy and capacities of the strong Taiwanese party-state in promoting export-oriented economic growth. Since the beginning of Taiwan's democratization, however, state-society relations have changed greatly. In the previous chapter, we analyzed changes in elite coherence and interagency conflicts within Taiwan's mainland affairs bureaucracies. The purpose of this chapter is to discuss the growing importance of social groups, especially business groups, and their influence on the state's formulation of cross-Straits economic policy.

In the early stage of cross-Straits interaction, the first businesses to venture into China were small and medium-sized firms. This trend changed in the early 1990s, when bigger companies and business groups began to initiate investment projects across the Taiwan Straits. In order to protect their interests in China, big businesses have utilized many different channels to influence state policymaking. Thus, state autonomy has been weakened, and a new form of state-business interaction has emerged. State-business relations have gradually developed into an alliance based on accommodation and cooperation.

The first part of this chapter will consist of a discussion of state-business relations during Taiwan's authoritarian era. This will be followed by an analysis of the rise of big business and the strategies it has used to influence economic policymaking in Taiwan. The investment activities of big business in China and the bargaining process with the state, as well as the implications of the new type of state-business relationship, will be discussed in the last part of the chapter.

State-Business Relations in Taiwan's
Authoritarian Era

The first two decades of Taiwan's postwar history was an era of state dominance over society. As a result of the February 28 Incident of 1947,[1] key Taiwanese nationalists were liquidated, driven into exile, or otherwise silenced. The KMT regime, controlled by mainlanders, was in full control of the island. Important social groups were incorporated into party organizations while state-controlled youth corps preempted independent student organizations and labor was also brought under state control.

The relationship between the Taiwanese party-state and local capitalists was greatly influenced by the land reform that began in 1949. One reason for the smooth implementation of the land reform was the lack of ties between the KMT and Taiwan's rural landlord class—which stood in contrast to the strong connections the party had with big business in China before 1949. Landlords were compensated by a combination of land bonds (70 percent) and government enterprise stock (30 percent). Although the rural reform undercut the basis of the landlords' power in the countryside, the method of compensation turned them into industrialists dependent on the goodwill of the regime.[2]

In addition to the destruction of the local elite and the undercutting of the landlord class, another factor contributing to the weakness of local capitalists was the size of the state-owned manufacturing sector (see Table 5.1). The state made extensive use of state-owned enterprises to realize its industrial aims, particularly in the field of intermediate and capital goods. Behind the state's desire to control the commanding heights of the economy was an unspoken political issue—Taiwanese-mainlander relations. Private-sector growth would inevitably strengthen the native Taiwanese, who then might use their economic power for political ends.[3]

Although the state-owned sector was still dominant, Taiwan's private firms also burgeoned in the late 1950s and early 1960s. As K. T. Li recalls, two factors led to the rise of the private sector: first, the state policy of "planned free economy" and the economic planners' preference for economic efficiency in the private sector; and second, U.S. intervention through the Agency for International Development (AID), which promoted economic liberalization and a free-market system in Taiwan.[4]

U.S. aid in the 1950s not only played a crucial role in stabilizing Taiwan's political and military situation but also enhanced private enterprise. Through the Council of United States Aid (CUSA), private industries received a large amount of assistance for development. As Chao Chi-chang argues, "most of today's big enterprises received direct or indirect American aid in the 1950s."[5]

TABLE 5.1   Distribution of Industrial Production by Ownership (Based on Value Added at 1981 Prices)

Year	Total	Distribution (%)	
		Private Sector	Public Sector
1952	100.0	43.4	56.5
1955	100.0	48.9	51.1
1960	100.0	52.1	47.9
1965	100.0	58.7	41.3
1966	100.0	61.8	38.2
1967	100.0	65.3	34.7
1968	100.0	68.9	31.1
1969	100.0	70.6	29.4
1970	100.0	72.3	27.7
1971	100.0	77.1	22.9
1972	100.0	78.7	21.3
1973	100.0	78.9	21.1
1974	100.0	78.1	21.9
1975	100.0	77.9	22.1
1976	100.0	77.5	22.5
1977	100.0	77.2	22.8
1978	100.0	78.5	21.5
1979	100.0	78.8	21.2
1980	100.0	79.1	20.9
1981	100.0	80.0	20.0
1982	100.0	79.9	20.1
1983	100.0	80.2	19.8
1984	100.0	81.2	18.8
1985	100.0	81.2	18.8
1986	100.0	82.5	17.5
1987	100.0	82.7	17.3
1988	100.0	81.9	18.1
1989	100.0	81.5	18.5
1990	100.0	81.3	18.7
1991	100.0	81.9	18.1
1992	100.0	82.0	18.0

SOURCE: *Taiwan Statistical Data Book 1993* (Taipei: Council for Economic Planning and Development, 1993), 84.

Through CUSA, the state controlled the distribution of funds to private businesses and thus controlled the businesses themselves. Composed of relevant ministers and chaired by the premier, CUSA had three main tasks: (1) to select aid projects and to procure and allocate aid-financed commodity imports, (2) to supervise the execution of aid projects, and (3) to maintain liaison with the U.S. AID Mission in China.[6] CUSA developed a good working relationship with American advisors in distributing American aid to both the public and private sectors.

The state's distributive capacity enabled it to maintain a patron-client relationship with business in Taiwan. The first wave of aid beneficiaries were capitalists in certain key industries, such as cotton textiles and flour milling. Most of these businesspeople were mainlanders from Shanghai or Shantung province, and they were able to apply to the government for allotments of AID-financed imported cotton or wheat. In the textile sector, an "entrustment" system was employed whereby the state supplied raw cotton, paid the workers' wages, and purchased the yarn. CUSA's Textile Subcommittee also controlled cloth weaving. The "entrepreneur" ran no risk and stood to make a fortune in a market where demand far outstripped supply. In the 1950s, American-aid cotton constituted 88 percent of cotton imports, and textile industries enjoyed a beneficial foreign exchange rate. The state even froze the establishment of new textile industries in the late 1950s to protect these mainlander capitalists in Taiwan.[7]

Having received shares in state enterprises in compensation for their land, Taiwan's biggest ex-landlords—the Japanese era collaborators— became the main beneficiaries when the state began to transfer these firms to private ownership in 1954. For example, the first posttransfer chairman of the Taiwan Cement Corporation was Lin Po-shou of the Panchiao clan, one of Taiwan's most powerful families. He was succeeded by Koo Chen-fu, son of Ku Hsien-yung, who had assisted the Japanese in their occupation of Taipei in 1895. This company enjoyed state protection and contracts. A seat on its board was considered to be a status symbol by later generations of Taiwanese capitalists.[8]

In the early start-up period, mainlander businesspeople depended on their ethnic background and access to technocrats within the regime to obtain benefits from American aid and state support. The state gave favorable treatment to mainlander-controlled textile industries and formed various joint ventures with mainlander capitalists. In an effort to ensure the success of their aid applications, mainlanders developed *guanxi* (personal connections) with the bureaucracy and even hired "American aid brokers" to get inside information about the aid system.[9]

At the same time, there were also a few Taiwanese who started their businesses in the 1950s and 1960s. In 1950, the state decided to privatize the polyvinyl chloride (PVC) industry through the AID program. After inspecting the state of his account in the Bank of Taiwan, the state picked a native Taiwanese rice merchant, Y. C. Wang, to establish the island's first PVC factory. From this small beginning, Wang built up Formosa Plastics and the Formosa Group and became one of the most successful businessmen in Taiwan.[10] Another entrepreneur, Lin Ting-sheng, built up his consumer electronics giant Tatung after receiving a substantial AID loan to assemble watt-hour meters.[11]

Native entrepreneurs also sought the cooperation of Taiwanese collaborators with the new regime for the sake of their political relations within the bureaucracy. Wu Hsiu-chi and Wu Tsuen-hsien, for example, cooperated with Wu San-lien, a Taiwanese journalist who had served the KMT in China and became the mayor of Taipei, to take over the government-initiated textile factories. On this basis, the Wu brothers developed the Tainan Group and the President Group, which later became one of the biggest enterprise groups in Taiwan. In 1964 the gas industry was opened to the private sector, and the Taipei Gas Company was established by Taiwanese businessman Wu Ho-su in a joint venture with Wu San-lien. Wu Ho-su also cooperated with Shieh Tung-min, another Taiwanese politician with a mainland background, to establish the Shin Kong Insurance Company in 1960.[12] Shin Kong and the Taipei Gas Company later provided the basis for Wu's Shin Kong Group.[13] Native entrepreneurs also developed relations with technocrats in the state hierarchy. For example, the Tsai brothers developed relations with the then minister of finance Yen Chia-kan to set up the Cathay Insurance Group, and Hsu Ching-teh developed relations with K. Y. Yin and K. T. Li to facilitate his establishment of Shihlin Electric & Engineering Corporation and the Nankang Tire Company.[14] All these enterprises developed into big business groups in the late 1970s.

More formal connections between government officials and business leaders were established through the state-sponsored industrial associations. At the top of the hierarchy were the Chinese National Federation of Industries and the General Chamber of Commerce of the Republic of China, representing the entire manufacturing and service sectors respectively, and the Chinese National Association of Industry and Commerce, whose membership included virtually all the elite business groups.[15] These associations were designed to function as an arm of both the state economic bureaucracy and the authoritarian party. The KMT used these associations to penetrate, organize, and demobilize various sectors of civil society. Elections for association officers were conducted by the Social Affairs Department of the KMT. Their leaders were usually handpicked by the paramount leaders Chiang Kai-shek and Chiang Ching-kuo to serve as official spokesmen for the business community. Hence, these associations lacked autonomy and therefore were relatively powerless as interest groups. Their organizations were quite loose, and their boards of trustees had never been reelected until the lifting of martial law in 1987.[16]

In brief, these industrial associations served as the instruments through which the KMT party-state exerted control over the private sector along corporatist lines. Behind this corporatist veil was a complex clientelist network that infiltrated the hierarchy of the intermediary institutions.[17] These associations were only what Juan Linz calls an "auxiliary government" or an "agent of implementation," not a "source of pressure." They were the transmission belt of the KMT party-state and were used to legitimize the state's economic policies.[18]

Some entrepreneurs participated directly in politics, but their influence was limited to the local level. The leaders of the core agencies of the economic bureaucracy were all government officials; there were no business representatives. During Taiwan's authoritarian years, the Executive Yuan Council never included any businesspeople. And by 1984, of the thirty-two members of the KMT Central Standing Committee, only two were local capitalists. In the early 1970s, limited electoral reforms allowed some businessmen into the Legislative Yuan, but they were still a small minority.[19]

Not only were the new capitalists and the industrial associations unable to influence state policies, but small and medium-sized businesses also lacked the necessary resources and skills for organizing group-based actions. These enterprises contributed more than 95 percent of Taiwan's exports; they were highly adaptable and would switch to different lines of business to accommodate to the changing international economic environment. This special kind of mobility encouraged business adjustment instead of collective bargaining and invited the "free-rider" phenomenon that was detrimental to effective collective action.[20]

To sum up, the state-business relationship in the authoritarian era was that of patron and client. There were no institutionalized channels through which business could articulate its interests, and electoral participation was limited to the local level. This situation was not changed until large-scale political reform was launched in the late 1980s.

State-Business Relations Since Democratization

One reason for the change in the patron-client relationship between state and business in the early 1980s was the rise of big enterprises and enterprise groups. In addition to their manufacturing profits from the domestic market, big enterprises accumulated capital through the booming stock and real estate markets in the mid-1980s. Through intermarriage and interinvestment, linkages among big enterprises became closer. More important, the policy of allowing the establishment of new private banks led directly to the cartelization of enterprises. The new Banking Law set the minimum capital requirement for a new bank at NT$10 billion (US$400 million), while the maximum investment for an individual enterprise was NT$5 billion (US$200 million).[21] So only the bigger enterprises were qualified to enter the banking business, and one direct result of this policy has been the merger of big enterprises and the formation of enterprise groups around the banks, similar to the *keiretsu* in Japan.

At the end of the 1980s, Taiwan's one hundred enterprise groups incorporated between seven and eight hundred enterprises and accounted for 34 percent of Taiwan's GNP. As many as 70 percent of them were owned by native Taiwanese.[22] This is in sharp contrast to the authoritarian era, when the state and mainlander capitalists controlled most of the big enterprises.

During the authoritarian era, political and economic resources were monopolized by the state. The state provided a highly protected domestic market for big enterprises and received political support in return. In the early 1980s, the state began to open its domestic market under pressure from the United States, which wanted to reduce its trade deficit with Taiwan. To compensate the big private businesses for the loss of protection, the government also opened state-monopolized industries to the private sector. Hence, the state was weakened and business could utilize its new financial power in its bargaining with the state. The patron-client relationship between the two was thus disrupted.

The business community also became more directly involved in politics in this period. The 1980s was a decade of rising social consciousness in Taiwan, and among the various mass movements that erupted at that time, the environmental and labor movements had the biggest impact on business. Antipollution activists launched a total of 108 protest campaigns in the years 1981–1988, most of them targeted at big enterprises such as Y. C. Wang's Formosa Plastics and the Du Pont chemical factory at Lukang.[23] Strikes and labor-management conflicts also became more frequent. New labor unions were formed that challenged the legitimacy of the existing KMT-sponsored organizations, and cross-regional and cross-factory federations were established. All of this drew the attention of the business community to the necessity of participating in the rule-making process. Getting involved in politics was the most direct way to protect their corporate interests.

Scholars have suggested various strategies that businesses can adopt to influence state policymaking from the stage of public-opinion formation right through to policy implementation.[24] In the case of Taiwan, big business does not perform too well in influencing public opinion. In one opinion poll conducted in 1991, 62 percent of the sample responded that "the prosperity of Taiwan is the fruit of the endeavors of all sectors of society, but big enterprise groups are the beneficiaries"; 56 percent agreed that "government officials and big enterprises are getting too close to each other"; 60 percent agreed that the corrupt linkage between legislators and business is "quite serious"; and 80 percent opposed big businesses using their financial power to influence public policymaking.[25] Hence, the main focus of big business's strategy is policymaking and implementation.

Political Donations

Enterprises invest money in election campaigns. Since 1992, 75 percent of the members of Taiwan's Legislative Yuan has been elected according to the single nontransferable vote (SNTV) system from medium-sized multi-member constituencies. This system pits candidates from the same party against one another and also encourages electors to vote for an individual candidate rather than a party. The multi-member constituencies mean that a candidate need only poll about 15 percent of the vote to get elected, a much smaller proportion than in a single-member constituency.[26] This system indirectly encourages vote buying, and to buy votes, or even to finance legal campaign activities, candidates need extra resources. During the 1992 Legislative Yuan election, the price of a vote was reported to range from NT$500 to NT$2,000.[27]

As campaign costs rise, donations from businesses become crucial. The Evergreen Group, for example, supports more than thirty legislators, including mainstream KMT and DPP members. The amount of donations ranges from US$20,000 to US$200,000, depending on the degree of intimacy.[28] In the 1993 election for county magistrates, the Hualon Group supported Ho Chih-huei, the successful candidate in Miaoli county, to the tune of US$40 million.[29] According to one estimate, 70 percent of candidates in the 1989 Legislative Yuan and county magistrate elections were supported by business groups.[30] Through their proxies in the legislature and local government, businesses get a return on their political investments in the form of probusiness laws, the rezoning of urban land to benefit the real estate market, and large construction contracts. In return, the lawmakers receive 10 to 15 percent commissions from the businesses concerned.[31]

Political Participation

Business leaders also participate directly in politics by standing for election. At the local level, the KMT has developed a patron-client relationship with local factions that are dominated by local enterprise groups. According to one study, in the 1992 Legislative Yuan election, 78.3 percent of all KMT nominees had factional backgrounds, and 82 percent of KMT candidates affiliated with local factions were elected.[32] Some second-generation business leaders, such as Oung Ta-ming of the Hualon Group and Wu Tong-sheng of the Shin Kong Group, were elected to the Legislative Yuan. Four members of the KMT Central Standing Committee elected in

1994 were leaders of enterprise groups—Koo Chen-fu of Koo's Group, Chen Tien-mao of the Kaohsiung Chen family, Kao Ching-yuan of the President Group, and Wang Yu-tseng of the China Rebar Group.[33] In brief, participating in elections and politics in general is the most effective way of protecting business interests. This channel of influence was not opened to Taiwan's businesses until the political reforms of the late 1980s.

KMT-Business Alliance

The third effective way for big businesses to establish political connections in Taiwan is for them to cooperate with KMT-owned enterprises. When the Nationalist government moved to Taiwan in 1949, only one KMT-owned company followed. But through the state's monopoly of resources and direct financial support from the state, KMT enterprises have expanded enormously over the past forty years. In 1994, the KMT owned seven holding companies and had investments in almost one hundred other companies (see Figure 5.1). The party's listed assets reached NT$36 billion (US$1.44 billion). This amount represents the book value of the seven holding companies but excludes cash and real estate held by the KMT Finance Committee. The market value of the KMT's corporate holdings is estimated to be around NT$100 billion (US$4 billion). In 1994, the KMT Business Management Committee expected to turn over some NT$4.1 billion (US$155 million) to the KMT Finance Committee for its annual operating budget, representing some 80 percent of operating income.[34]

KMT enterprises were in the habit of forming joint ventures with state enterprises. These ventures included stock brokerages and investment, insurance, and construction companies. Since 1988, the KMT Finance Committee has shifted toward joint ventures with big private-business groups, such as Koo's Group, Y. C. Wang's Formosa Group, and the Wu family's Shin Kong Group.[35] Hence, a tripartite alliance consisting of state enterprises, the KMT, and private firms was formed. This has created a symbiotic relationship: Business interests are protected by the political umbrella, and the KMT gains the financial resources it needs to support its campaign expenses.

Business Associations

The operation of the business associations also changed in the late 1980s. The boards of trustees of the two major associations, the Chinese National Federation of Industries and the General Chamber of Commerce of the Republic of China, were reorganized in early 1991. Under the leadership of Koo Chen-fu, and more recently his son, Jeffrey Koo, the Chinese

FIGURE 5.1 KMT Enterprises

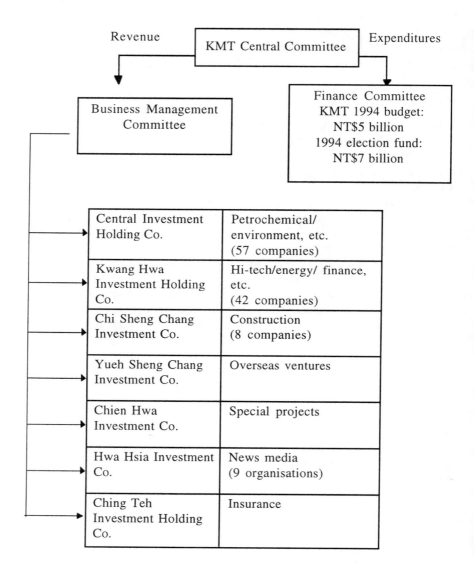

SOURCE: Revised from Julian Baum, "The Money Machine," *Far Eastern Economic Review* (August 11, 1994):63.

National Association of Industry and Commerce (CNAIC) has become the principal bridge between the state and business.[36] The heads of Taiwan's top enterprises account for 43 percent of the CNAIC's fifty-eight member board of trustees, compared to 21 percent of the board of the Chinese National Federation of Industry and 5 percent of the General Chamber of Commerce, which are more representative of smaller enterprises.[37] Moreover, the CNAIC includes leaders of state enterprises, semiofficial trade organizations, and KMT enterprises.[38] Through its monthly breakfast meetings with high-ranking economic bureaucrats and the personal influence of the Koo family, the CNAIC is expected to play a role similar to that of Keidanren in Japan. It could help to create consensus within the business community and persuade the government to adopt policies that accord with business interests.[39] The Research Association of Industry and Commerce (RAIC), a business association organized by second-generation entrepreneurs, is a new corporate group established since the lifting of martial law. Through its five branches and by means of its good relations with the KMT, the RAIC mobilizes its young members to participate in election campaigns and thereby influence government policies.[40]

To sum up, big corporations have utilized a variety of channels to influence state policymaking. Big business finances the party and the state, and the state provides the necessary political protection in return. As big business penetrates the Chinese market, Taiwan's economic policymaking with regard to China will become a prolonged process of state-business accommodation.

Big Business and Taiwan's Cross-Straits Economic Policy

In the early period of economic interaction across the Taiwan Straits, most Taiwanese economic transactions with China were conducted through smuggling or investments by small enterprises focusing on labor-intensive industries.[41] The average value of investment projects was below US$1 million. In Xiamen for example, individual Taiwanese enterprises investing a maximum of US$1 million constituted 74.6 percent of Taiwanese investors in 1988 and 64 percent in 1989.[42] Most of the investments were in labor-intensive industries, and 70 percent were export oriented.[43]

This situation began to change in 1993. According MAC statistics, the average value of individual Taiwanese investments in China rose from US$365,000 in 1990–1992 to US$779,000 in 1993, an increase of 2.13 times.[44] In 1995, the average value of investments by Taiwan listed companies was more than US$6.6 million.[45] The second wave of Taiwanese investment in China, beginning after Deng Xiaoping called for a faster pace of economic reform during his tour of southern China in early 1992, was characterized by the participation of larger enterprises and enterprise groups as well as small, independently owned companies. These bigger firms were not so export oriented, being interested in manufacturing for China's domestic market. They adopt more gradual and long-term strategies to create a division of labor between their Taiwan headquarters and their manufacturing centers in China. Investing in China became a crucial part of their globalization plans.[46]

Aside from their own development strategies, Taiwan's big business groups find that they are being "pushed" into China by the smaller firms. As small- and medium-scale "downstream" manufacturers transfer their factories to China, the big enterprises that supply them with raw materials and components feel a pressure to move also. Taking the petrochemical industry as an example, with more than 80 percent of downstream manufacturers of apparel, toys, and footwear having moved to China, midstream plastics and rubber manufacturers come under pressure to move too, in order to cut down on transportation and labor costs. And if upstream industries do not follow suit, the midstream industries will shift to cheaper Korean or even Chinese suppliers. If this happens, it will disrupt the vertical division of labor in Taiwan's petrochemical industry. One company that has come under pressure in this way is the Nan Ya Plastics Corporation, part of the Formosa Group.

Political Connections and Mainland Investments

Big enterprises utilize their well-organized political networks on both sides of the Straits to protect their interests. The case of the President Group, which has one of Taiwan's biggest investment projects in China, is a good example. The "Tainan Gang," of which the President Group is an offshoot, began as a textile shop during the Japanese occupation of Taiwan. The loose grouping of interlocking shareholders and bloodlines eventually came to include some twenty-odd firms. The group launched its internationalization drive in the late 1980s, and in 1991 it paid US$355 million to buy Wyndham Biscuits, the third-largest cookie maker in the United States.[47] In 1994, the President Group ranked sixth among Taiwan's top one hundred enterprise groups, with annual sales of more than US$3 billion.[48] Investment projects in China are an important part of President's internationalization plans.

The chairman of the President Group, Kao Ching-yuan, has very good connections with the government, although he has never participated directly in elections.[49] Kao inherited the political connections of the "Tainan Gang," and in particular, he has developed personal relationships with President Lee Teng-hui, Premier Lien Chan, and James Soong, the governor of Taiwan province, through his support for many government projects.[50] In response to Lee Teng-hui's call for businesses to invest in Southeast Asia, Kao led a large group of enterprise representatives on a study tour of the region, and he invested US$80 million in government aviation industry projects. In January 1994, he was elected chairman of the Chinese National Federation of Industries, and in August he became a member of the KMT's Central Standing Committee.[51]

The President Group's investments in China were facilitated by Beijing's new policy of opening its domestic market to foreign firms in order to win entry to the General Agreement on Tariffs and Trade (GATT). In 1992, the group reached an agreement to set up food factories in China. The Chinese counterpart agreed to a maximum export rate of 30 percent, with at least 70 percent of President's products being sold on the domestic market.[52] In December 1992, on the day of the third meeting of the KMT's Thirteenth Central Committee, Kao flew to Shanghai, where he signed the US$12 million contract.[53] By the end of 1993, Kao had invested about US$60 million in China. In the future, Kao plans to invest in every province of China, and most of these new ventures will be solely owned by the President Group.

As the chairman of the Chinese National Federation of Industries, a trustee of the Straits Exchange Foundation, and a KMT Central Standing Committee member, Kao is in a good position to urge the government to lift restrictions on investment in China. He has also been a strong advocate of direct transportation across the Taiwan Straits and advancement into the "medium-term stage" of cross-Straits relations as mentioned in the "Guidelines for National Unification." His political connections on both sides of the Taiwan Straits give Kao Ching-yuan a persuasive voice in policymaking.

The most frequently mentioned example of state-business connections is the Evergreen Group. The group's president, Chang Jung-fa, is a Japanese-trained native Taiwanese entrepreneur. His political network spans both the KMT and the DPP and includes technocrats and lawmakers. Chang also recruits retired (but not too old) high-ranking bureaucrats to serve in his enterprises. His close relationship with President Lee is well known.[54]

There were loud accusations of unfair advantage in mid-1991, when the Evergreen Group successfully applied to establish Taiwan's first private international airline. EVA Airways obtained waivers from the Ministry of Transportation and Communications allowing it to begin service with only leased aircraft and to hire foreign pilots. But the issue that aroused the most controversy was a land lease agreement that enabled EVA to construct a hangar and maintenance terminal at Chiang Kai-shek International Airport. The ministry's revision of the airport's master plan to accommodate EVA was attacked by Legislator Yok Mu-ming and other nonmainstream politicians.[55]

The EVA affair is a good illustration of Chang's ability to influence public policymaking. The affair also indirectly led to the resignation of two ministers of transportation and communication in succession, but after the deal was done, the deputy director of the Civil Aeronautics Administration "retired" and became vice president of EVA.[56]

The Evergreen Group did not begin to form plans for investing in China until 1993. In early 1994, Chang began to urge the government to lift the ban on direct transportation across the Straits. In June, the MOEA's Investment Commission approved a US$6 million plan by the Evergreen Group to build a container depot in Shanghai. The group also gained approval for the establishment of branch offices in Shanghai and Xiamen.[57] There are huge potential profits for Evergreen companies in the China market in such areas as air transportation, shipping, and construction. Considering the Evergreen Group's political connections, it may exert sufficient pressure to get the state to open direct transportation for domestic carriers and to adopt more liberal trade policies toward China.

Business Associations and Mainland Investment

The big corporations also work through business associations to influence Taiwan's China policy. Since 1990, the Chinese National Federation of Industries and the General Chamber of Commerce of the ROC have sent annual delegations to China. It was the then chairman of the Chinese National Federation of Industries, Hsu Sheng-fa (also a member of the KMT Central Standing Committee and vice chairperson of the Straits Exchange Foundation) who, after returning from a fact-finding tour of China with an MOEA official in November 1993, incurred the wrath of the MAC by calling for closer economic interaction across the Straits and a change in current policy.[58]

In the interagency conflicts between the MAC and the MOEA, the General Chamber of Commerce of the ROC has also taken the MOEA's side. After meeting Premier Li Peng and President Jiang Zemin in Beijing, Chamber of Commerce chairman You-cheng Wang said that Taiwanese businesspeople are quite capable of weighing the risks of investing in China and that the government should not intervene too much in the booming cross-Straits economy. On economic issues, he asserted, the MAC should respect the opinion of the MOEA.[59]

The business associations also participate directly in the policymaking process. In March 1993, the MOEA established a Mainland Affairs Committee, headed by Vice Minister Yang Shih-chien, to take responsibility for planning and evaluating the MOEA's economic policy toward China. Also included on the committee are the secretaries-general of the Chinese National Federation of Industries, the General Chamber of Commerce of the ROC, the China External Trade Development Council (CETRA), and the Textile Association. This was the first time that the government in Taiwan had formally included business representatives in the China policymaking process.[60]

The business associations play the role of a bridge between the state and the business community when the MOEA is deciding whether to open up new categories of Chinese investments or imports. The ministry seldom turns down recommendations from business and professional associations for additions to be made to the list of permitted categories, and decisions on special cases are made only after a painstaking process of consultation between the state and business interests (see Figures 5.2 and 5.3).

KMT Enterprises

It was only in mid-1994 that KMT-owned enterprises were permitted to invest in China. However, most managers of these companies had visited China several times before then. In 1993, the KMT's Business Management Committee approved an investment project with the Beijing-controlled but Hong Kong-based APT Satellite Company. This was carried out through the Hong Kong–based Kwang Hua Development and Investment, a US$20 million joint venture between the KMT and Taiwan's Ruentex Group.[62]

Joint ventures in which the KMT controls less than 50 percent of the stock were free to do business with China before 1994. For example, the Chien Tai Cement Company, of which the KMT has a 30 percent share, invested US$20 million in China, and the CTIC Corporation, another KMT joint venture, has various petrochemical projects there. As Liu Tai-ying, the chairman of the KMT's Business Management Committee, has said, most KMT-owned enterprises are "well-prepared to advance into mainland China."[63]

The Y. C. Wang Shock

In June 1990, after several visits to China, Y. C. Wang, the president of the Formosa Group, announced a plan to build a US$5 billion petrochemical complex on Haicang Island near Xiamen in Fujian province. The Formosa Group wanted the complex to include an oil refinery producing petroleum and oil as well as naphtha for its two naphtha crackers. Thirty-four

FIGURE 5.2   Review Process for Mainland Investments

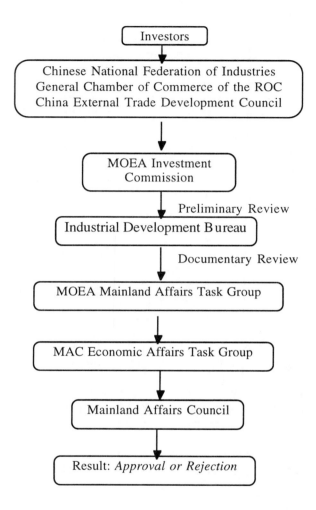

SOURCE: *Talu touzi huo jishu hezuo shenqing xuke xuzhi* (Guide to Applying to Invest or Carry Out Technical Cooperation on the Mainland) (Taipei: Investment Commission, Ministry of Economic Affairs, 1993), 7.

FIGURE 5.3   Review Process for Imports from China

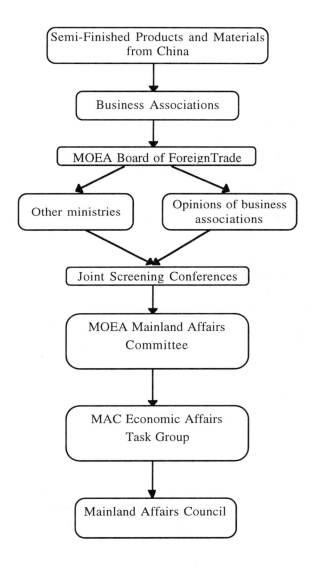

SOURCE: Kao Koong-lian, *Liang'an jingmao xiankuang yu zhanwang* (Current Status and Prospects of Cross-Straits Economic Relations) (Taipei: Mainland Affairs Council, 1994), 46.

mills were to be built to process the ethylene into plastics. The Chinese government would provide a loan worth US$5 billion and invest US$7 billion in improvements to Haicang's infrastructure.[64]

The Haicang project came as a major shock to policymakers in Taiwan. The US$5 billion investment was about equal to Taiwan's total domestic investment between 1980 and 1989. There was also the prospect that it would attract mid- and downstream petrochemical enterprises to move to China and undermine the whole petrochemical industry in Taiwan. Moreover, Wang's project was a direct challenge to Taiwan's ban on direct investment in China.

This affair opened a new era of state-business bargaining in Taiwan. In late 1991, under pressure from high-ranking government officials, Y. C. Wang declared that the Haicang project was "postponed," but not canceled. At the same time, he was urging the government to renegotiate terms for a new petrochemical complex in Taiwan that had been stalled because of high land costs and opposition from environmentalists.[65] Wang hinted that the main reason why the Haicang project had stalled was the Chinese authorities' failure to fully satisfy his demands.[66] Wang was signaling to both sides that the door was still open and he would ally with whichever side offered the best deal.

In June 1992, the government approved Wang's project to build a US$2.2 billion naphtha cracker in Mailiao, Taiwan. At almost the same time, the Chinese decided to give Wang more preferential terms for his Haicang project. These included allowing the Formosa Group to procure low-priced oil, to establish its own bank in Xiamen, and to operate its own cargo ships, and guaranteeing a high ratio of domestic sales—almost everything Wang had demanded.[67]

The Taiwan government still insisted on blocking the Haicang project, but in way of compensation, it made a deal with Wang to increase the size of his Mailiao project. Known locally as the "sixth naphtha cracker," the US$9.5 billion project was then three times larger than when it was first proposed. The project's location—on the opposite side of the Taiwan Straits to China—would enable it to serve the factories that had transferred from Taiwan to southern China. The Formosa Group also struck a deal with the government under which the company agreed to fund much of the zone's infrastructure in return for long-term low-cost financing of US$5.4 billion. Other concessions included a five-year tax break, low-cost water supplies, and a government agreement to fund port development and other costs.[68]

Y. C. Wang's interest in China did not disappear after he struck the Mailiao deal. In 1993, Wang announced that he was discussing another proposal to supply products exclusively to the Chinese domestic market. If the deal went through, he would build new factories on the Yangtze

River near Shanghai.[69] The Formosa Group's indirect sales to China in 1993 totaled approximately US$6 billion,[70] and in August 1994 it was reported that First International Computer, a Formosa subsidiary and the biggest motherboard maker in the world, would be producing up to 150,000 motherboards and up to 70,000 personal computers per month on a large site near Shanghai.[71]

Business-Legislature Connections

As mentioned earlier, big corporations donate money to legislators or participate directly in elections to guarantee their business interests. In Taiwan, there are few rules governing the extracurricular activities of lawmakers, and some have become wealthy after winning their seats. Many legislators are directors of companies and foundations aligned with their particular groups, leaving them open to accusations of undue financial gain.[72]

The close relationship between business and legislators creates a unique situation in Taiwan's legislature. A large number of lawmakers skip most legislative sessions and concentrate only on proposals and budgets that involve the interests of their factions or financial backers. Although the KMT will enforce discipline where politically sensitive legislation is concerned, it avoids dissuading legislators from going their own way when it comes to economic or financial matters.[73] Many legislators choose which committees to sit on for reasons of personal financial interests, the most popular committees being those of economics, finance, and home and border affairs, because they often involve major tax, bond, and stock market decisions.[74]

Cross-Straits economic interaction and related business matters is a popular area of specialization for Taiwan's legislators. Lawmakers with business backing are eager to speed up the pace of cross-Straits trade. According to data from the Legislative Yuan Information Center, during the 85th to 89th sessions of the legislature (1991–1992), mainland policy was the most popular interpellation topic.[75] In 1992, during the passage through the legislature of the Statute Governing Relations Between People of the Taiwan Area and the Mainland Area, the first law governing cross-Straits relations, legislators raised record numbers of proposals and amendments, and a record number of executive-legislative coordination meetings was held.[76]

The legislature managed to enhance its oversight of cross-Straits economic policy when, under pressure from KMT legislators, a joint meeting of the judicial, domestic, and legal affairs committees passed an amendment stating that the executive needs the consent of the Legislative Yuan before opening direct trade and transportation with China. The ruling party also incorporated several amendments initiated by the opposition party into the final draft.[77] In 1993, the Legislative Yuan further enhanced its powers by passing an amendment to the statute, giving itself the power to investigate related executive orders promulgated by the executive branch.[78]

However, the Legislative Yuan's influence on China policymaking should not be exaggerated. Legislators can oversee the executive only through oral and written interpellations. These actions could attract public attention to cross-Straits economic relations, but they do not function as an effective method of supervision. Legislators can neither participate in decisions regarding permitted areas of investment nor get involved in negotiations with China.[79] More important, until 1995 there was no mainland affairs committee in the Legislative Yuan. China-related policies and regulations were reviewed by different committees, such as the economic affairs committee, the domestic affairs committee, the foreign affairs committee, and so forth.[80] These structural factors have also hampered the Legislative Yuan's capacity to supervise China policymaking.

By contrast, many legislators have successfully established their own "China connections." From 1990 to 1993, more than half of all legislators, both KMT and DPP, visited China.[81] At first, lawmakers went as tourists or to visit relatives, but since 1991 their visits have mainly been for the purpose of establishing business connections. Legislators with aviation or shipping connections at home seek contacts with related bureaucrats in China to arrange future shipping and aviation routes; those supported by the petrochemical industry visit oil fields and establish connections with state-owned enterprises; those supported by the lumber industry go to the northeast to investigate the possibility of developing its huge forest resources. Yet other legislators go to China to negotiate investment projects on their own behalf or survey the domestic market for future investment.[82]

Legislators have also set up foundations to promote cross-Straits interaction. These foundations play the role of an intermediary between Taiwanese businesspeople and their mainland counterparts and help solve conflicts and collect business information. They are not arms and agents of the state. On the contrary, the government always feels that they are "going too far" and that they violate state policies. The special status of legislators as both business representatives and politicians gives them the capacity to build a "bridge" across the Taiwan Straits.

Although the legislative body cannot participate directly in decisions regarding permitted categories of investment, legislators can lobby the executive branch quite effectively. Legislators backed by the cement industry, for example, lobbied the economic bureaucrats to transfer investment in cement from the prohibited to the permitted list. Their efforts were unsuccessful, but the government agreed to block imports of foreign cement as compensation. The effectiveness of these lobbying efforts depends on the political status and financial power of the individual legislators concerned.

Conclusion

State-business relations in the 1990s are very different from the patron-client relations of the authoritarian era. This change is also reflected in the area of cross-Straits economic interaction.

The case of Y. C. Wang's Haicang project and the case of the cement industry mentioned previously provide good examples of state-business conflict and cooperation. Investment projects in China have been useful chips with which to bargain with the state in Taiwan. The ultimate target of big business is domestic economic benefits, and the possibility of investment in China serves as a tool to achieve this goal. In Wang's case, financial strength gives him the power to manipulate the governments on both sides of the Straits. Although he finally opted to locate his project in Taiwan, he still has plans to expand into China. From this perspective, Taiwan's cross-Straits economic policy is a prolonged process of accommodation between big business and the state rather than a matter of autonomous state decision-making.

Another notable feature of state-business relations is the rise in the influence of business associations. The top associations have all been reorganized since the democratization process was started, and they enjoy more autonomy than before. The leaders of these associations have established personal connections with state bureaucrats and have been recruited into the highest decisionmaking body of the KMT. Their voice is heard also in decisions concerning investment in China. However, the participation of top business associations in the policymaking process is still different from the corporatist style of policymaking implemented in some European countries.

One important characteristic of corporatism is the institutionalization of interest representation.[83] But in Taiwan, interest integration and articulation between the state and big business are more personal than institutional. The top business associations lack the capacity to integrate labor and employee interests down to the grassroots level, and channels of communication between their leaders and the state are based on personal access or connections. Hence, whereas Koo Chen-fu, as chairman of the Straits Exchange Foundation, could represent Taiwan in negotiations with his mainland counterpart, his Chinese National Association of Industry and Commerce could do nothing to prevent the Formosa Group's Y. C. Wang and other business leaders from rushing into the China market.

Since democratization, the business-legislature linkage has become closer than before, though the legislature's capacity to influence Taiwan's China policy is limited. The role of individual legislators is not to initiate new cross-Straits economic policies; instead, the legislator's job is to see that the interests of his or her backers are protected.[84] The individual legislator plays the role of a "broker," promoting and protecting business interests in China, and serves as a link between the state and business. Most of these functions are performed outside the legislative institutions, not in the regular process of lawmaking.

Compared to its insulation from local business penetration in the authoritarian era, the state now has a closer alliance with domestic capitalists. Since democratization and economic liberalization were initiated, the domestic elite has gained control of most political and economic resources. This creates a congruence, rather than separation, between political power and economic interests. The allocation of political resources is not decided by autonomous edicts issued by the supreme leader but through a conciliation and cooperation process between the state and business. In the case of cross-Straits economic policymaking, business groups have actually proved to be a valuable resource for the Ministry of Economic Affairs in its struggle with the Mainland Affairs Council on such issues as direct transportation and direct trade with China.[85] All of these examples demonstrate that the making of Taiwan's China policy is no longer an autonomous state action. Businesspeople provide financial resources to political parties and ally with bureaucracies to promote specific policies. In return, businesspeople gain political protection for their economic interests.

Although the KMT has formed various alliances with local factions and big business groups, the influence of business interests on the ruling party is limited by the fact that the KMT has a separate financial resource—its own huge business empire. KMT-controlled enterprises could also be a useful vehicle for manipulating and adjusting economic activities according to state policies. Thus, while KMT joint ventures have rushed into the booming China market, KMT-controlled enterprises and holding companies have only recently been permitted to invest there.

To sum up, the influence of big business on Taiwan's cross-Straits economic policymaking has been on the rise since the mid-1980s. As they adopted strategies of internationalization and China gradually opened its domestic market, individual enterprises and business groups began to initiate large-scale investment projects in China. These firms influence economic policymaking by providing financial support for lawmakers, allying with KMT enterprises, establishing personal connections with officials, and bargaining with the state through business associations. However, business influence is not articulated through institutionalized channels. The business associations and the legislature have not developed into powerful institutions for collective bargaining as have those in the pluralist states. State-business alliances are based more on personal relations, and their effectiveness depends on the business's financial capacity and its degree of access to the political elite. Looking to the future, Taiwan's business interests in China will become more comprehensive, and the influence of the legislature and the business associations will become more institutionalized. As state autonomy is challenged by these institutionalized social forces, a more corporatist style of cross-Straits policymaking may emerge in Taiwan.

Notes

1. For a detailed discussion of the February 28 Incident, see Lai Tse-han, Wei Wou, and Ramon Myers, *A Tragic Beginning* (Stanford: Stanford University Press, 1992).

2. Stephan Haggard, *Pathways from the Periphery* (Ithaca: Cornell University Press, 1991), 82. For land reform, see Hsiao Hsin-huang, *Government Agricultural Policies in Taiwan and South Korea* (Taipei: Academia Sinica, 1981).

3. Haggard, *Pathways from the Periphery*, 88.

4. Kang Lu-tao, *Li Guoding koushu lishi* (An Oral History of K. T. Li) (Taipei: Cho-yueh, 1993), chapter 6.

5. Chao Chi-chang, *Meiyuande yunyong* (Using American Aid) (Taipei: Linking, 1985), 111.

6. Neil H. Jacoby, *U.S. Aid to Taiwan* (New York: Praeger, 1966), 61.

7. Wen Hsin-ying, *Jingji qijide beihou* (Behind the Economic Miracle) (Taipei: Independence Evening News Press, 1980), 262; Thomas Gold, *State and Society in the Taiwan Miracle* (New York: M. E. Sharpe, 1986), 70.

8. Gold, *State and Society in the Taiwan Miracle*, 71.

9. Hsia Chi-yueh, "The Use of American Aid Over the Past Ten Years," *Caizheng jingji yuekan* (Journal of Finance and Economy [Taipei]) no. 12 (1959):6.

10. Kang, *Li Guoding koushu lishi*, 86–87.

11. For a detailed introduction to the Tatung Group, see Yu Chang-shan, "Lin Ting-sheng: Tatung's Protector," *Tianxia zazhi* (Commonwealth Magazine) (August 1994):154–174.

12. Shieh Tung-min became governor of Taiwan province in the 1970s; in 1978 he was chosen by Chiang Ching-kuo to be the first native Taiwanese vice president.

13. Huang Ching-hsin, *Banshijide fendou: Wu Huoshi xiansheng koushu zhu-anji* (Business as a Vocation: The Autobiography of Mr. Wu Ho-su) (Taipei: Yun-cheng, 1990), 204–207.

14. Hsu Jui-shih, *Zhengshang guanxi jiedu* (An Analysis of State-Business Relations) (Taipei: Yuan-liu, 1991), 66–67.

15. Chu Yun-han, *Crafting Democracy in Taiwan* (Taipei: National Policy Research Center, 1992), 34.

16. Hsu, *Zhengshang guanxi jiedu*, 58–59.

17. Chu, *Crafting Democracy in Taiwan*, 135.

18. Juan Linz, "An Authoritarian Regime: Spain," in *Mass Politics: Studies in Political Society*, ed. Frik Alardt (New York: Free Press, 1970), 299; Chou Yu-jen, *Zhengzhi yu jingjizhi guanxi* (The Relationship Between Politics and the Economy) (Taipei: Wu-Nan, 1993), 94.

19. Chien-kuo Pang, *The State and Economic Transformation: The Taiwan Case* (New York: Garland, 1992), 113.

20. Mancur Olsen, *The Logic of Collective Action* (Cambridge: Harvard University Press, 1965).

21. Christina Liu, "Liberalization and Globalization of Financial Markets," in *Taiwan's Enterprises in Global Perspective*, ed. N. T. Wang (New York: M. E. Sharpe, 1992), 142; Wei Chi-lin, "The Relationships and Development Trends of Taiwan's Enterprises Big and Small," in *Qiye zhengfu yu shehui yantaohui* (Proceedings of Seminar on Enterprises, Government, and Society) (Taipei: National Policy Research Center, 1992), 3–9.

22. Wei, "The Relationships and Development Trends," 3–5.

23. Hsiao Hsin-huang, "The Rise of Social Movement and Civil Protests," in *Political Changes in Taiwan*, ed. Cheng Tun-jen and Stephan Haggard (Boulder: Lynne Rienner, 1992), 60.

24. Mike H. Ryan, Carl L. Swanson, and Rogene A. Buchholz, *Corporate Strategy, Public Policy and the Fortune 500* (Oxford: Basil Blackwell, 1987), 45.

25. Hsu, *Zhengshang guanxi jiedu*, 55.

26. For the SNTV system, see J. A. A. Stockwin, "Political Parties and Political Opposition," in *Democracy in Japan*, ed. Takeshi Ishida and Ellis S. Krauss (Pittsburgh: Pittsburgh University Press, 1989), chapter 5; Shelley Rigger, "The Impact of Institutional Reform on Electoral Behavior in Taiwan" (paper delivered at annual meeting of the American Political Science Association, Washington, D.C., September 1993).

27. *China News* (Taipei), December 15, 1992, 1. Cited in Andrew J. Nathan, "The Legislative Yuan Elections in Taiwan: Consequences of the Electoral System," *Asian Survey* 23, no. 4 (April 1993): 429.

28. *Xin xinwen* (The Journalist) (Taipei), September 11, 1993.

29. Ibid., December 11, 1993.

30. Chou, *Zhengzhi yu jingjizhi guanxi*, 113.

31. Lin Chi-yen, legislative assistant, interview with the author, August 12, 1994.

32. Huang Teh-fu, "Modernization, Electoral Competition, and Local Factions in Taiwan" (paper delivered at the 1993 Annual Meeting of the American Political Science Association, Washington, D.C., 1993), 7.

33. *Zhongguo shibao* (China Times) (Taipei), August 27, 1994.

34. *Lianhe bao* (United Daily News) (Taipei), August 8, 1994; Julian Baum, "The Money Machine," *Far Eastern Economic Review*, (August 11, 1994):62–67.

35. Chen Shih-meng et al., *Jiege dangguo zibenzhuyi* (Deconstructing Party-State Capitalism) (Taipei: Cheng-she, 1991), 72.

36. Koo Chen-fu's formal positions include president of the board of trustees of the Straits Exchange Foundation, member of the KMT Central Standing

Committee, and honorary president of the Chinese National Association of Industry and Commerce.

37. Chou, *Zhengzhi yu jingjizhi guanxi*, 122.

38. Ibid.

39. For Keidanren, see Glen Fukushima, "Corporate Power," in Ishida and Krauss, *Democracy in Japan*, 255–281; F. M. Scherer, *Industrial Market Structure and Economic Performance* (New York: Rand McNally, 1980).

40. *Zhongshi zhoukan* (China Times Magazine) (September 11, 1994):22–23.

41. N. T. Wang, "Taiwan's Economic Relations with Mainland China," in Wang, *Taiwan's Enterprises in Global Perspective*, 61.

42. The average level of investment by foreign firms is US$1.5 million. See Kao Charng and Tsai Hui-mei, "On Cross-Straits Investment and Trade Relations," in *Liang'an guanxi yu dalu zhengce* (Cross-Straits Relations and Mainland Policy), ed. Huang Tien-chung and Chang Wu-yueh (Taipei: Wu-Nan, 1993), 342.

43. Yin Tsun-i, "The Theory and Practice of Cross-Straits Industrial Cooperation," in *Disanjie haixia liang'an guanxi yantaohui lunwen* (Proceedings of the Third Annual Meeting on Cross-Straits Relations) (Ningbo, China: 1993), 2.

44. *Yuanjian* (Global Views) (Taipei), August 15, 1994, 32.

45. *Jingji ribao* (Economic Daily News) (Taipei), July 24, 1995.

46. *Lianhe bao*, January 5, 1993.

47. Lincoln Kaye, "Recipe for Success: Taiwan's President Group Looks to the U.S. to Maintain Sales Growth," *Far Eastern Economic Review* (March 21, 1991):54–57.

48. *Tianxia zazhi*, June 1994, 99.

49. Russell Flannery, "New Rule Book for Taiwan Firms," *Asian Business* (March 1991):9.

50. According to one report, Kao can visit or telephone these leaders directly in their offices. See Tan Shu-chen, "An Interview with Kao Ching-yuan," *Xin xinwen*, August 1, 1993, 66–72.

51. *Zhongguo shibao zhoukan* (China Times Weekly), March 27, 1994, 24; *Zhongguo shibao*, August 27, 1994.

52. Urban Lehnar, "China: Native Intelligence," *Asian Wall Street Journal* (December 10, 1993).

53. Ho Ya-wei, "Kao Ching-yuan: From Preparation to Action," *Yuanjian*, December 12, 1992.

54. For a detailed discussion of Evergreen's political connections, see Chou Tsui-ju, "The Political-Business Relations of the Evergreen Group," *Xin xinwen*, June 17, 1991, 20–26.

55. Julian Baum, "Ever Upwards," *Far Eastern Economic Review* (June 20, 1991):81–82.

56. *Xin xinwen*, April 6, 1991, 46.

57. *Asian Wall Street Journal* (August 22, 1994).

58. *Shibao zhoukan*, January 13, 1994, 16–18.

59. Ibid.

60. *Lianhe bao*, April 4, 1993.

61. Chen Jung-yuan, staff member of Economic and Trade Services Department of the Straits Exchange Foundation, interview with the author, August 14, 1994.

62. Julian Baum, "The Money Machine," 66.

63. *Lianhe bao*, December 14, 1993.

64. Jonathan Moore, "The Emperor Speaks," *Far Eastern Economic Review* (June 28, 1990):82.

65. Ibid.

66. *Financial World* (July 19, 1994):56.

67. *Gongshang shibao* (Commercial Times) (Taipei), June 5, 1992.

68. Julian Baum, "Taking the Plunge," *Far Eastern Economic Review* (April 22, 1993):75.

69. Ibid.

70. *Zhongguo shibao zhoukan* (China Times Business Week), April 24, 1994, 24.

71. *Business Week* (August 15, 1994):91.

72. Julian Baum, "Turbulence Ahead," *Far Eastern Economic Review* (February 13, 1992):25.

73. Chu, *Crafting Democracy in Taiwan*, 145.

74. Jim Hwang, "The Cabernet Sauvignon Theory of Lawmaking," *Free China Review* (March 1994):17.

75. *Qingnian ribao* (Youth Daily News) (Taipei), August 24, 1992.

76. *Zhongyang ribao* (Central Daily News) (Taipei), April 4, 1992.

77. *Zhongguo shibao*, September 24, 1992.

78. Yang Tai-shun, *Lifayuan diaochaquanzhi yanjiu* (Investigation Power of the Legislative Yuan) (Taipei: Democracy Foundation, 1993), 2.

79. Hsu Kun-yao, legislative assistant to legislator Lai Ying-fang, interview with the author, August 5, 1994.

80. Hwang, "The Cabernet Sauvignon Theory of Lawmaking," 17.

81. *Zhongguo shibao*, July 26, 1993.

82. Hsu Kun-yao, legislative assistant to legislator Lai Ying-fang, interview with the author, August 4, 1994.

83. Philippe Schmitter, "Still the Century of Corporatism?" in *The New Corporatism*, ed. Fredrick Pike and Thomas Stritch (Notre Dame, Ind.: University of Notre Dame Press, 1974), 93–94; Douglas Chalmers, "Corporatism and Comparative Politics," in *New Directions in Comparative Politics*, ed. Howard Wiarda (Boulder: Westview Press, 1985), 56–80.

84. Michael Mezey proposes three kinds of legislatures: the policymaking model, the representation model, and the system-maintenance model. Taiwan's Legislative Yuan since 1992 seems to fit the representation model. The predemoc-ratization Legislative Yuan only possessed the functions of system maintenance and legitimization. For a detailed discussion, see Michael Mezey, *Comparative Legislatures* (Durham, N.C.: Duke University Press, 1979).

85. See Chapter 4.

6

Governing Cross-Straits Economic Relations

In the previous chapter, we examined one important aspect of the state-centered approach to the study of political economy—state autonomy and state-business interaction. In this chapter, we will highlight another crucial aspect of this approach: the regulative capacity of the state. The study of state capacity focuses on formal rules, policy instruments, and informal routines. All these formal and informal procedures are put into the larger context of the entire social-economic situation in order to examine the capacity of the state and the institutional goals of state actions.

The state's regulative policies with regard to foreign economic relations compete with the market mechanism in the international arena. The state meets two major challenges: the profit-seeking activities of businesspeople and economic interdependence among trading states. The state needs to accommodate domestic social forces on the issue of trade and investment and to protect national interests through deliberate designs in order to enhance its competitive edge and increase international cooperation. The "strong state" initiates policies that are the autonomous actions of the state elite, leads the market, and adjusts the economic structure to accommodate the changing international environment. At the same time, the dynamic business community seeks to evade state regulations and maximizes its benefits according to the market mechanism. The booming China market attracts trade and investment from Taiwan and Hong Kong and thus creates a relationship of economic interdependence among these three economies. This interdependent relationship, based on economic benefits, acts as a further constraint on autonomous state regulation of cross-Straits trade and investment.

In this chapter, we will discuss the capacity of the Taiwanese state to regulate the market mechanism and the activities of Taiwanese business-people in China. First of all, the legal framework of trade and investment will be compared with actual business performance. Second, the state's efforts to lead and impede the market motivation of private firms will be analyzed. Finally, the emergence of the "Greater China Economic Circle" and its impact on economic interdependence and state action in this region will be examined.

Economic Regulations

Taiwan's economic policy toward China follows the mercantilist line of trade regulation. Whereas the liberal school of international trade emphasizes comparative advantage and the market mechanism as the major sources of economic change, mercantilism and economic nationalism focus on the state as the predominant actor and use foreign economic relations as an instrument to achieve political interests and national security. In brief, economic nationalism of the mercantilist variety emphasizes the political framework of economic activities and recognizes that markets must function in a world of competitive groups and states.[1] Hence, regulating trade and investment for the sake of national interests can be legitimized as autonomous state actions.

For reasons of national security, direct economic linkages with China are currently prohibited in Taiwan. All the economic activities across the Taiwan Straits must be conducted through a third party, normally Hong Kong. Regulations in this area may be categorized as those governing imports, exports, and investment.

Import Regulations

Taiwan opened indirect trade with China in 1987. According to the 1988 "Principles Governing the Indirect Import of Goods from Mainland China," only twenty-nine categories of agricultural and industrial materials were allowed to be imported.[2] Since 1988, Taiwan has used a system of "positive listing," according to which the government specifies which categories of goods may be imported from China. As economic interaction across the Taiwan Straits has increased, the Taiwanese government has added more items to the list.

The 1993 "Regulations Governing Trade Between Taiwan and Mainland China" set out three principles for allowing goods to be imported from China: (1) the goods shall not pose any threat to national security; (2) they shall not have any adverse effect on related industries in the domestic market; and (3) they shall have the positive effect of sharpening the competitive edge of local products in the international market.[3] Before September 1994, about 2,637 different items were permitted to be imported to Taiwan from China.[4]

Export Regulations

For the regulation of exports to China, Taiwan uses the looser "negative listing" system. In the 1993 "Regulations Governing Trade Between Taiwan and Mainland China," three categories were included on the prohibition list: (1) rare animals and plants; (2) high-tech products; and (3) commodities with an impact on national security. According to the Mainland Affairs Council, only 103 items, or 1.3 percent of Taiwan's commodities, are prohibited export items.[5]

Investment Regulations

The four-decade-long ban on Taiwanese investment in China was eased in 1991. According to the 1993 "Regulations Governing Investments and Technical Cooperation with Mainland China," investment activities must be conducted in an indirect way. "Indirect investment" may be conducted through four channels: (1) through a branch of a Taiwan company established in a third country; (2) through investment in another company located in a third country; (3) through a company in a territory outside China; or (4) through indirect remittance.[6]

Indirect investments in China are divided into three categories—those on the permitted list, those on the prohibited list, and special cases. With due regard to national security and domestic economic development, the government approves investment projects if they can meet the following four criteria: (1) they do not compete with Taiwan's domestic industries in the international market; (2) they are labor-intensive in nature; (3) they use raw materials produced in China; and (4) the line of business would be uncompetitive if continued in Taiwan.[7]

On the prohibited list are agricultural projects that would compete with the domestic agricultural sector; high-tech and defense projects, prohibited for national security reasons; and the service sector, banking, securities, futures, and insurance, which are prohibited in order to control business activities and the outflow of capital to China.

For the "special case" category, there are four requirements: (1) investors must continue their investment projects in Taiwan; (2) investment projects in China must not exceed the size of the company's current investments in Taiwan; (3) investment projects in China must not have any negative impact on Taiwan's national security or economic development; and (4) investment projects must be approved by the company's shareholders and board of directors.[8]

To sum up, the Taiwanese state tries to intervene directly in economic interaction with China by means of strict economic regulations. The

TABLE 6.1   Commodity Trade Between Taiwan and China via Hong Kong, 1981–1995 (in US$ million)

Year	Total Trade with China		Exports to China		Imports from China	
	Amount	Growth Rate (%)	Amount	Growth Rate (%)	Amount	Growth Rate (%)
1981	459.33	47.61	384.15	63.49	75.18	–1.35
1982	278.47	–39.37	194.45	–49.38	84.02	11.76
1983	247.69	–11.05	157.84	–18.83	89.85	6.94
1984	553.20	123.34	425.45	169.55	127.75	42.18
1985	1,102.73	99.34	986.83	131.95	115.90	–9.28
1986	955.55	–13.35	811.33	–17.78	144.22	24.43
1987	1,515.47	58.60	1,226.53	51.18	288.94	100.35
1988	2,720.91	79.54	2,242.22	82.81	478.69	65.67
1989	3,483.39	28.02	2,896.49	29.18	586.90	22.61
1990	4,043.62	16.08	3,278.26	13.18	765.36	30.41
1991	5,793.11	43.26	4,667.15	42.36	1,125.95	47.11
1992	7,406.90	27.86	6,287.93	34.73	1,118.97	–0.62
1993	8,688.98	17.31	7,585.42	20.63	1,103.56	–1.38
1994	9,809.50	12.90	8,517.20	12.30	1,292.30	17.40
1995	11,457.00	16.70	9,882.80	16.03	1,574.20	21.80

SOURCE: *Liang'an jingji tongji yuebao* (Monthly Report on Cross-Straits Economic Relations) (Taipei: Mainland Affairs Council, June 1995), June 1995, 20; *Liang'an jingmao tongxun* (Newsletter of Cross-Straits Economy) (Taipei, Straits Exchange Foundation), March 1996, 47.

state's capacity to regulate and reverse the trend toward closer economic interaction across the Taiwan Straits can be estimated by examining the real performance and activities of Taiwanese businesspeople in China.

Economic Activities of Taiwanese Businesspeople in China

The regulative policies of the Taiwanese government have failed to deter profit-seeking Taiwanese businesspeople from rushing into the China market. As will become obvious, a large portion of economic transactions across the Taiwan Straits are actually conducted directly, in defiance of government regulations. The state also lacks effective policy instruments to regulate business motivation and behavior.

The Statistical Gap in Cross-Straits Economic Interaction

According to official Hong Kong customs statistics, trade between Taiwan and China via Hong Kong was worth US$11.45 billion in 1995 (see Table 6.1). These official statistics, however, are not an accurate reflection of the flow of trade between the two sides of the Taiwan Straits. As Taiwan's minister of economic affairs P. K. Chiang has indicated, more than 60 percent of all cross-Straits trade is conducted directly.[9] According to the estimate of the Board of Foreign Trade of the Ministry of Economic Affairs, total trade in 1993 would reach US$13.83 billion if transit cargo and air transshipment figures excluded by Hong Kong were added to the total.[10]

According to Ma Tien-tse, secretary-general of the Chinese Marine Research Association (Taiwan), indirect trade through Hong Kong is conducted in three different ways: (1) commodities are shipped from Taiwan to Hong Kong, pass through Hong Kong Customs, and are then transferred to other ships heading for China; (2) commodities are exported from Taiwan to Hong Kong, and then transferred by land to China—the Hong Kong Customs will have import records but no export records for indirect trade through this route; (3) exports from Taiwan are transferred in Hong Kong waters to another cargo vessel heading for China—the cargo neither enters the harbor nor passes through Hong Kong Customs. Of these three channels for trade via Hong Kong, only the first one is included in official statistics on the reexport trade issued by the Hong Kong Customs.[11]

Hence, official statistics from Hong Kong reflect only part of the bilateral trade value. The real trade value may be calculated as follows. The difference between the value of Taiwan's exports to Hong Kong as shown in Taiwan Customs data and Hong Kong's imports from Taiwan as shown in Hong Kong Customs data (the former being larger than the latter) represents the value of commodities transferred to China without passing through Hong Kong Customs. In 1995, this figure was US$9.54 billion (see column 4 in Table 6.2).

One may also assume that a large portion of Taiwan's exports to Hong Kong are transferred to China overland, because there is no way that a market the size of Hong Kong could absorb all the imports it receives from Taiwan. In 1995, Hong Kong imported about US$16.57 billion worth of commodities from Taiwan, of which US$9.8 billion was registered as being reexported to China. That leaves US$6.77 billion worth of goods officially remaining in Hong Kong. But according to the estimate of Professor Sung Yun-wing of the Chinese University of Hong Kong, approximately 82 percent of this—or US$5.55 billion worth in 1995—would actually have been transferred to China.[12] Since trade via Hong Kong does not represent the entire value of trade between Taiwan and China (some of it is conducted through other places, such as Japan and South Korea), this estimate of 82 percent will be used here instead of the Mainland Affairs Council's estimate of 70 percent (US$4.74 billion in 1995).[13]

Hence, if we add the figures in columns 4 and 5 of Table 6.2 to the official figure for Taiwan's indirect exports to China via Hong Kong (see

TABLE 6.2   Adjusted Taiwan Exports to China, 1981–1995 (in US$ million)

	Taiwan's exports to China via HK	Taiwan's exports to HK	HK's imports from Taiwan	Taiwan's exports minus HK's imports	HK's imports from Taiwan transferred to China	Taiwan's estimated real exports to China
Year	(1)	(2)	(3)	(4)=(2)–(3)	(5)=((3)–(1))x82%	(7)=(1)+(4)+(5)
1981	384.20	1,897.00	1,896.40	0.60	1,240.00	1,624.80
1982	194.50	1,565.30	1,570.10	–4.80	1,127.99	1,317.69
1983	157.80	1,643.60	1,600.00	43.60	1,182.60	1,384.00
1984	425.50	2,087.10	2,217.50	–130.40	1,469.44	1,764.54
1985	986.80	2,539.70	2,682.40	–142.70	1,390.39	2,234.49
1986	811.30	2,921.30	3,072.80	–151.50	1,854.43	2,514.23
1987	1,226.50	4,123.30	4,275.10	–151.80	2,499.85	3,574.55
1988	2,242.20	5,587.10	5,682.40	–95.30	2,820.96	4,967.86
1989	2,896.50	7,042.30	6,606.90	435.40	3,042.53	6,374.43
1990	3,278.30	8,556.20	7,439.90	1,116.30	3,412.51	7,807.11
1991	4,667.20	12,431.30	9,605.00	2,826.30	4,049.00	11,542.50
1992	6,287.90	15,416.00	11,156.30	4,259.70	3,992.09	14,539.69
1993	7,585.40	18,454.90	12,0047.20	6,407.707	3,658.68	17,651.78
1994	8,517.20	21,263.00	13,757.70	7,505.30	4,297.21	20,319.71
1995	9,882.80	26,121.10	16,572.60	8,548.50	5,485.63	24,916.93

SOURCE: *Liang'an jingji fenxi baogao* (Monthly Report on Cross-Straits Economic Relations) (Taipei, Mainland Affairs Council), June 1994, 33; March 1995, 24; *Minzhong ribao* (Popular News), June 25, 1994; *Gan Ao yuebao* (Hong Kong-Macau Monthly) (Taipei, Mainland Affairs Council), March 1996, 24; author's own calculation.

Table 6.2, column 1), the amount for 1995 comes to US$24.9 billion. There is also a big gap between the Taiwan and Chinese figures for Taiwanese investments in China (see Table 6.3). One reason for this is that Chinese data is based on the "negotiated" rather than the "contracted" value of investment, which makes the Chinese figure rather high. However, the negotiated value better reflects the way Taiwan businesspeople have broken through the legal barriers to investment in China erected by the Taiwan government. The main reason for this large gap in investment data between Taiwan and China is that many Taiwanese businesspeople conduct "direct investment" without the approval of their government, or else they underreport the value of their investments.[14]

To sum up, a substantial portion of cross-Straits economic interaction is conducted directly. The huge statistical gap between the official data and the actual value of trade and investment indicates that the Taiwanese

TABLE 6.3   Taiwanese Investment Projects in China, 1991–1994 (in US$ million)

Year	Approved by Taiwan		Approved by China	
	No. of Projects	Amount	No. of Projects	Amount
1991	237	$174.158	3,800	$3,450.000
1992	264	$246.992	6,430	$5,547.900
1993	9,329	$3,168.411	10,948	$9,970.000
1994	934	$962.21	6,247	$5,397.000
Total	10,764	$4,551.771	27,425	$24,364.900

SOURCE: *Liang'an jingji fenxi baogao* (Monthly Report on Cross-Straits Economic Relations) (Taipei, Mainland Affairs Council, June 1994 and March 1995), 45, 62 (June), 30 (March).

state's capacity to execute its policy of indirect trade and investment is weak.

The General Trend of Taiwanese Investment in China

Taiwanese investment in China has exhibited a number of general trends. First of all, the geographical location of investment projects has gradually expanded from the coast toward the inland provinces and from the south to the north. According to Chinese statistics, by the end of August, 1994, there were 21,863 Taiwanese firms spread over twenty provinces in China (see Table 6.4).

The scale of Taiwanese investment projects has changed from small-sized to medium- and large-sized. The average value of new investment projects is higher than before, and Taiwanese are either increasing their investments in existing projects or upgrading their factories.[15] In 1994, only 23 percent of Taiwanese investment projects were valued at more than US$1 million, compared to 37 percent in 1995.[16]

Different industries are also tending to use different investment strategies. For those aiming at foreign markets, sole ownership is a popular way to reduce costs; and investing in the coastal areas of China is convenient for shipping exports. For those with more interest in the huge China market, joint ventures with Chinese state enterprises are more beneficial because they are permitted to sell at least 30 percent of their total output on the domestic market.[17] However, unhappy experiences of cooperation with Chinese partners have persuaded Taiwanese businesspeople to shift gradually to sole ownership. By the end of 1995, 53 percent of Taiwanese-invested enterprises in China were wholly Taiwanese owned.[18]

Taiwanese investment projects, which in the past involved simply the transfer of old, outdated equipment, are now more likely to involve the use of completely new production lines. There has also been a shift from

TABLE 6.4   Distribution of Taiwanese Enterprises in China

Province	Number of Taiwanese Firms
Jiangsu	4,030
Guangdong	3,459
Fujian	3,215
Shandong	2,140
Zhejiang	1,800
Liaoning	978
Sichuan	972
Hainan	958
Hubei	814
Henan	621
Hunan	500
Jiangxi	460
Guangxi	420
Heilongjiang	386
Anhui	370
Shanxi	248
Jilin	207
Yunnan	120
Gansu	112
Xinjiang	53

SOURCE: Straits Exchange Foundation data, August 1994.

labor-intensive assembly and processing industries to higher level capital-intensive industries.[19] In the early stages, Taiwanese investors engaged mainly in quick-return, short-term projects in rented factory premises. In recent years, they have tended to make long-term investments with a duration of twenty to thirty years, and they are more likely to lease land to build their own factories.[20]

In general, Taiwanese investors are making a profit in China. According to a 1992 survey, about 80 percent of Taiwanese enterprises in China were profitable.[21] Another survey conducted in 1993 indicated that 55 percent of Taiwanese businesspeople in China were making money and 24 percent were breaking even; 59 percent planned to increase their investments.[22] Only about 39 percent of Taiwanese businesspeople were making money according to a survey conducted in 1995, while 24.6 percent were breaking even and 30 percent were registering losses.[23]

Taiwanese investors tend to adopt a flexible strategy. They are ready to adjust to the changing economic environment in China and they resist political intervention from Taiwan. The Taiwanese government adopts various measures to regulate business activities, but these do not have a major impact on Taiwan's profit-seeking businesspeople.

Policy Instruments to Regulate Taiwanese Businesspeople

In addition to legal restrictions on trade and investment, the Taiwanese state has adopted various measures aimed at regulating Taiwan's business relations with China.

Investment Registration. Generally speaking, the Taiwan government's policies lag behind the real situation of cross-Straits economic interaction. According to the Statute Governing Relations Between People of the Taiwan Area and the Mainland Area, all the investment activities in China must be approved in advance by the Taiwan government and all investments made before the promulgation of the statute should have been registered within six months. Violators are liable to a fine of up to NT$3 million (US$120,000).[24] From the legal perspective, the investment regulations are very strict and the punishment is severe.

However, as the preceding analysis shows, the number of actual investment projects far exceeds the official figure. Moreover, according to an October 1993 report, the Ministry of Economic Affairs had never punished any businesspeople for investing illegally in China.[25] In early 1994, the government issued the Regulations Governing Business Activities in Mainland China, which revised and simplified the investment screening process. But as expected, few businesspeople have bothered to register with the MOEA.[26]

Financial and Monetary Instruments. Financial policies have been a useful tool for the Taiwanese state to use to manipulate economic growth and development. These include financial policies for exports and strategic industries as well as the setting up of specialized banks and selective credit-control policies. These special sectors of the economy are provided with special medium- and long-term low-interest loans. The interest rate difference between these strategic loans and the prime rate is around 1.75–2.75 percent.[27]

These financial instruments can also be used to control Taiwanese investments abroad. In allocating loans to stimulate domestic investment, the Central Bank of China gives priority to firms with investment projects in Taiwan's domestic market.[28] On the other hand, the Central Bank tends to limit credit to firms investing in China. Even though these firms may have MOEA clearance to invest in big projects in China, the maximum amount of foreign exchange they are allowed by the Central Bank is US$3 million. This limit has forced some firms to revise or cancel their projects while others obtain foreign exchange through illegal channels.[29]

Taiwanese investors in China obtain most of their capital from Taiwan, since Chinese banks have little enough cash available anyway, and it is difficult for Taiwanese businesspeople to get loans from the local branches of Hong Kong or other foreign banks because they usually require land ownership or other collateral. Hence, on average, 56 percent of their capital comes from Taiwan, 25 percent from China, and 11 percent comes from a third country.[30] Furthermore, since Taiwanese banks were not allowed to establish branch offices in China before the end of 1995, Taiwanese investors have been forced to obtain their loans from domestic banks in Taiwan, which are subject to government controls.

However, the effectiveness of the government's financial tools is greatly reduced by the existence of other channels for obtaining capital in Taiwan. Taiwan firms obtain a substantial portion (more than 20 percent) of their capital on the black market, which the government is incapable of controlling through financial means.[31]

Moreover, Taiwanese investors can bring their capital out of Taiwan by purchasing travelers checks or transferring foreign exchange earned from exports. Exporters sometimes retain their foreign exchange to invest in China. According to Citibank in Taipei, the amount of foreign exchange retained by Taiwanese exporters increased from US$2.89 billion in 1987 to US$24 billion in 1991.[32] A large portion of this foreign exchange flows directly into China, and the Central Bank of China is not able to control this capital outflow.

Investment Protection.   As demonstrated in Chapter 5, although investment in China by big enterprises is gradually gaining momentum, small and medium-sized firms constitute the majority of Taiwanese businesses there. These dynamic firms adopt flexible policies to survive and expand in the often unfavorable Chinese environment.

The Taiwanese government seeks to assist and guide Taiwanese enterprises in China in two different ways. The first is to urge China to sign an investment protection agreement with Taiwan, because from Taiwan's perspective current PRC regulations provide uncertain protection for the property and rights of Taiwanese businesspeople. Beijing has so far resisted these urgings, claiming (1) that since Taiwan is part of China, Taiwanese businesspeople are protected by PRC domestic law,[33] (2) since Taiwan does not allow direct investment in China, there is no such thing as "Taiwanese investment," and (3) an investment protection agreement should be mutual, and Chinese firms are not permitted to invest in Taiwan.[34]

The investment protection agreement fell through because it was a political rather than an economic issue. The PRC insisted that Taiwanese investment was a "special kind of domestic investment" and should therefore be regulated by domestic law. From Beijing's perspective, the Taiwanese government was trying to use an economic issue to enhance its political status in relation to the PRC.

Another measure adopted by the Taiwanese government to protect its investors was the establishment of an interministerial group whose main tasks are to provide business information and to establish Taiwanese busi-ness associations in China. By mid-1994, sixteen such associations had been set up in major Chinese cities.[35] However, the operations of these associations are largely controlled by the Taiwan Affairs Office of the PRC's State Council, which "recommends" people to serve as their deputy directors. Taiwan's Straits Exchange Foundation plays very little part in the daily operation of the Taiwanese business associations. Although the SEF is supposed to serve as an intermediary between the government and business and to solve businesspeople's problems, its Chinese counterpart, the Association for Relations across the Taiwan Straits, is reluctant to cooperate. Of the 140 inquiries submitted by the SEF in the first half of 1994, only 14 received replies from ARATS.[36]

Hence, the real situation is that Taiwanese businesspeople need to establish their own network of connections (*guanxi*) and solve their own problems through the "back door." As one Taiwanese businessman has remarked, policies made in Taipei and cross-Straits negotiations or agree-ments actually help very little on the ground; what really controls the daily life of the Taiwanese investor is the local city or county government in China, or even a minor official in a small government department.[37] According to a survey conducted by a private company in Taipei, 78 per-cent of Taiwanese investors find "their own way" to solve problems in China, 13 percent contact Chinese officials, and only 6 percent solve prob-lems through the Taiwanese business associations.[38]

In conclusion, most Taiwanese firms in China manage their own busi-ness outside state control. Neither financial and monetary instruments nor business associations have a major impact on their daily operations. What really controls their activities is their assessment of the economic benefits to be gained from the huge China market.

Cross-Straits Economic Connections and the Prospects of a "Greater China Economic Circle"

Taiwan's Ties with the Coastal Areas of China

As the preceding analysis shows, the majority of Taiwanese investments are concentrated in the coastal areas of China, especially Guangdong, Jiangsu, and Fujian provinces. Since Deng Xiaoping's "southern tour" in early 1992, Taiwanese investments have rapidly expanded to cover the entire coast and some parts of the interior.

Between January and September 1993, 482 projects involving direct Taiwanese investment were approved in Shanghai alone. The projects involved contracted capital of US$430 million, surpassing the total for the previous five-year period both in terms of the number of projects and the value of investment. In 1995, Jiangsu became the Chinese province with the largest number of Taiwan-funded enterprises. Up to mid-1995, Jiangsu had attracted US$12 billion in Taiwanese investments.[39]

Taiwanese firms in the coastal areas operate their businesses in quite a unique way. Generally speaking, cross-Straits trade is investment-driven; that is, it is to a large degree an extension of Taiwanese investment activities in China.[40] This can be seen most clearly from Taiwan's exports to China, which form the bulk of cross-Straits trade. Materials, parts and accessories, and machinery and equipment constitute around 70 percent of these exports, and a large portion of these producer goods are imported by Taiwan-funded enterprises. It is estimated that 54 percent of the materials and 75 percent of the machinery and equipment needed by Taiwanese businesses in China are imported from Taiwan.[41] This situation gives Taiwanese firms more autonomy and insulates them from external political interference.

The bulk of China's foreign trade is conducted through Hong Kong, which is itself a major market for Chinese products in addition to being an entrepôt center for reexports to and from China. It was estimated that at one time Hong Kong contributed more than 70 percent of China's foreign exchange reserves.[42] Most Hong Kong firms have investments in the Pearl River Delta area of Guangdong province. However, some of these so-called Hong Kong investments are in reality conducted by Taiwanese. Since Taiwan forbids direct investment in China, many Taiwanese investors register as Hong Kong, American, or Japanese businesspeople through their overseas branches, and "Hong Kong" is the identity of choice among Taiwanese investing in Guangdong. It is believed that about 35 percent of all "Hong Kong investments" in China are in fact Taiwanese investments, and from 1991 to 1994, 70 percent of China's foreign direct investment came from Taiwan and Hong Kong.[43] Thus, Taiwan, Hong Kong, and the coastal areas of China have developed an interdependent relationship in trade and investment.

Trade between Taiwan and Hong Kong is also on the rise. Since 1993, Hong Kong has become Taiwan's third largest trade partner, after the United States and Japan, and in the first seven months of 1995, Hong Kong took first place in terms of exports.[44] As the preceding analysis shows, a substantial portion Taiwan's exports to Hong Kong have flowed into China. Thus, Taiwan's economic influence upon Guangdong and its vicinity has been indirect, and the distinction between Taiwanese and Hong Kong businesspeople, and between Taiwan and Hong Kong interests in Guangdong, is blurred.

To sum up, Taiwan, Hong Kong, and the coastal provinces of China have become closely connected and economically interdependent. From an optimistic perspective, economic interdependence could ease political tensions and promote trade liberalization in this region. The creation of a "Greater China Economic Circle" could also lay the foundation for future political cooperation and integration. In this situation, the Taiwanese state does not need to use political instruments to regulate cross-Straits economic interaction; the market mechanism and economic benefits provide the most effective protection for Taiwanese investments in China.

The Impact of the "Greater China Economic Circle"

The creation of the Greater China Economic Circle (GCEC) has its economic benefits and strategic necessities. The economic rationale for the GCEC lies in the complementarity of factor endowments throughout the region, especially among the coastal provinces of southern China, Taiwan, and Hong Kong. In recent years, the continued economic expansion of Hong Kong and Taiwan has been constrained by shortages of land and labor and the associated pressures of high rents and wages. Whereas the unemployment rate in these regions was well under 2 percent during the second half of the 1980s, that of Guangdong and Fujian was growing by 2.85 and 3.35 percent, respectively. This meant that there was plenty of cheap labor and land available for overseas entrepreneurs who were prepared to relocate their operations to southern China.[45]

Economic integration between Taiwan and China is also encouraged by the trend toward economic regionalization since the end of the Cold War. In the post–Cold War world, hegemony no longer depends on nuclear predominance; leadership depends instead on the ability to provide stable international monetary, financial, and trading conditions in the new world order. "Geoeconomics" seems to be replacing geopolitics in the global struggle for power.[46] The international economy is divided into three large blocs: Western Europe, North America, and East Asia. Together, they account for more than 80 percent of the world's GNP.[47] With the establishment of the North American Free Trade Agreement (NAFTA) and the European Union, a kind of "managed liberalization" has emerged in these two regions. And in East Asia, a Greater China economy may emerge to counter the hegemonic ambitions of Japan.

A rather optimistic view of the GCEC is that it will act as a kind of "Chinese common market." According to Cheng Chu-yuan, such a common market would probably involve: (1) the elimination of all trade barriers and the initiation of direct trade between Taiwan and China; (2) full protection of Taiwan investments in China and freedom for Taiwanese to transfer their profits out of the country; (3) stabilization of the Renminbi-New Taiwan Dollar-Hong Kong Dollar exchange rate; (4) a free flow of capital and commodities, but restrictions on movements of labor because of the small size of Hong Kong and Taiwan; (5) the formation of transnational corporations in the fields of petrochemicals, aerospace, computers and telecommunications, shipbuilding, etc., in which members of the Chinese common market have a comparative advantage; and (6) joint exploration of natural resources in the interior of China, cooperation in scientific research, and joint action to prevent the degradation of the environment.[48]

As for the economic scale of the GCEC, the combined foreign trade value of the Chinese economic region, comprising China, Taiwan, and Hong Kong, topped that of Japan in 1993. The foreign trade of the GCEC accounted for 8.5 percent of the world's total, compared to 8.04 percent for Japan.[49] On the basis of the current GNP of Taiwan, Hong Kong, and China, and its growth rate over the past ten years, James Hsiung has estimated that by 2010 the combined GNP of the GCEC will reach 17.4 percent of the world total. If we take account of the complementary and interactive effects among these three economic entities, the GNP should be larger still, and probably in excess of Japan's 19.4 percent of the world total.[50]

However, more pessimistic views of the GCEC abound. From an economic perspective, the intraregional trade volume in the GCEC is still less than the volume of trade with outside countries. In 1992, intraregional trade accounted for only 20.3 percent of the total, compared to 63.4 percent for the European Community and 37.3 percent for what is now NAFTA.[51] This means that the benefits of economic complementarity would be offset by possible competition in the international market. The total foreign trade volume after economic integration would likely be significantly lower than the "combined" value of the three economic entities. Furthermore, China shows a reluctance to play the role of labor and national resource provider, thus becoming what some Chinese leaders have termed a "colonial economy." Premier Li Peng once said that China did not welcome "sunset industries" from Taiwan and Hong Kong. These feelings would weaken cooperation and reduce the benefits of economic integration in the region.

Internationally, the creation of a GCEC might arouse fear of a "Chinese Gang" among neighboring states such as Japan and the countries of the Association of Southeast Asian Nations (ASEAN). According to Oranski's theory of "rear-end collision," an equilibrium and balance of economic power increases the danger of an economic war by tempting both sides to believe that they could win.[52] Though the ASEAN countries already perceive the danger of a rising Chinese economic force, Japan will also be threatened by this Chinese economic bloc. The creation of a GCEC may therefore produce economic instability instead of cooperation in the Asia-Pacific region as a whole.

Hence, the economic integration of "Greater China" is problematic from an economic perspective. As Peter Robson argues, the main difference between economic integration among developed countries and that among developing countries is that in the case of the latter, the prospective gains from integration are based on the "emergent" rationalization of production rather than the existing structures of production. Future gains or losses are unclear, and the production structures of individual countries also keep changing. It is difficult for participants to estimate accurately the impact of such far-reaching arrangements. Thus, for integration among developing countries to succeed, it seems that a more deliberate approach of bargaining and negotiations is necessary, compared to that found in advanced economies.[53] Such a process must be based on mutual trust and consensus, elements lacking in the relationship between Taiwan and China.

Economic Interdependence and Dependence

Economic integration is a special kind of arrangement that formalizes existing patterns of interdependence. Functionalists have long argued that successful collaboration in less contentious and more functional areas fosters mutual confidence that will gradually "spill over" into political areas. Thus, the integrative forces unleashed by exchanges in trade and communication can promote expectations and institutions of interdependence and joint decisionmaking. These forces also undermine exclusive national sovereignty and make it difficult for a state to undertake unilateral political action. Eventually, integration may lead to amalgamation.[54]

Functionalists and neofunctionalists pay special attention to the "quantity" of communication, cultural exchange, and trade transactions in their analyses of interdependence between Taiwan and China.[55] However, these are the "prerequisites" of interdependence, not proof of the existence of interdependence itself. As John Garnett correctly indicates, interdependence is a matter of the "quality," not the quantity, of exchanges. Whether an increasing number of transactions between states produces greater interdependence depends entirely on the nature of the transactions.[56] What is important is, first, whether these ties are costly to break, and, second, whether the relationship of interdependence is "asymmetric." Asymmetric interdependence may increase the vulnerability of the weaker side instead of enhancing mutual benefits.

Taiwan's economic relationship with China is asymmetric. Taiwan's economic dependence on China has been on the rise in the past few years. In particular, Taiwan's degree of dependence on the Chinese market for its exports has far surpassed the "warning line" of 10 percent set up by the Ministry of Economic Affairs (see Table 6.5). At the same time, Taiwan's

TABLE 6.5   Economic Interdependence Between Taiwan and China, 1981–1995 (in percentages)

Year	Share of Exports to China in Taiwan's Total Exports	Share of Trade with China in Trade Trade	Share of Exports to Taiwan in China's Total Exports	Share of Trade with Taiwan in China's Total Trade
1981	7.19	3.54	0.34	0.77
1982	5.93	3.00	0.38	0.73
1983	5.51	2.85	0.40	0.69
1984	5.79	3.12	0.49	0.69
1985	7.27	4.17	0.42	0.56
1986	6.31	3.70	0.46	0.62
1987	6.66	3.71	0.73	0.89
1988	8.19	4.07	1.01	0.99
1989	9.61	4.88	1.12	1.18
1990	11.62	5.78	1.23	1.61
1991	15.15	7.49	1.57	1.99
1992	17.85	8.75	1.32	9.46
1993	20.78	10.21	1.20	9.58
1994	21.83	12.42	1.53	9.36
1995	21.49	12.27	n.a.	n.a.

SOURCE: *Liang'an jingji fenxi baogao* (Monthly Report on Cross-Straits Economic Relations) (Taipei, Mainland Affairs Council), June 1994, 33 and 37; March 1995, 29; *Taiwan Statistical Data Book 1993* (Taipei: Council for Economic Planning and Development, 1993), 190; Table 6.2; *Zhonghua minguo Taiwan diqu jinchukou maoyi yuebao* (Monthly Statistics of Exports and Imports, Taiwan Area, The Republic of China) (Taipei, Ministry of Finance), February 1996, 16, 65; *Zhonghua minguo Taiwan diqu Guomin jingji dongxiang tongji jibao* (Quarterly National Economic Trends, Taiwan Area, The Republic of China), Taipei, Executive Yuan, February 1996, 50.

trade dependence on the United States is declining (see Table 6.6). The value of Taiwan's trade with China, especially exports, will soon surpass that of Taiwan's trade with the United States. Furthermore, without its trade surplus with China, Taiwan would actually have a trade deficit overall (see Table 6.7). All of these data illustrate the importance of the China market in Taiwan's international trade.

As for the structure of exports and imports to and from China, Taiwan's major imports from the other side of the Straits are agricultural and industrial materials, such as Chinese herbal medicines, corn and cooking oil, marine products, minerals, and raw materials for textiles. On the other hand, Taiwan's exports to China are mainly in the form of manufactured products and semimanufactured goods, including synthetic fiber materi-

TABLE 6.6   Taiwan's Trade with China, the United States, and Japan as Percentage of Total Trade, 1981–1995 (in percentages)

Year	China	U.S.A.	Japan
1981	3.54	36.10	11.00
1982	3.00	39.40	10.70
1983	2.85	45.10	9.90
1984	3.12	48.80	10.50
1985	4.17	48.10	11.30
1986	3.70	47.70	11.40
1987	3.71	44.10	13.00
1988	4.07	38.70	14.50
1989	4.88	36.30	13.70
1990	5.78	32.40	12.40
1991	7.49	29.30	12.10
1992	8.75	28.90	10.90
1993	10.21	24.81	19.85
1994	12.42	23.75	19.62
1995	12.27	21.91	20.17

SOURCE: *Liang'an jingji fenxi baogao* (Monthly Report on Cross-Straits Economic Relations) (Taipei: Mainland Affairs Council), June 1994, 33, 37; March 1995, 28; *Taiwan Statistical Data Book 1993* (Taipei: Council for Economic Planning and Development, 1993), 203; *Zhonghua minguo Taiwan diqu jinchukou maoyi yuebao* (Monthly Statistics of Exports and Imports, Taiwan Area, The Republic of China) (Taipei, Ministry of Finance), February 1996, 16, 65; *Zhonghua minguo Taiwan diqu Guomin jingji Dongxiang tongji jibao* (Quarterly National Economic Trends, Taiwan Area, The Republic of China), Taipei, Executive Yuan, February 1996, 50.

als and products, polystyrene and its copolymers, polyvinyl chloride, electrical machinery, and machinery and equipment for industry.[57]

Taiwan's economic dependence on China greatly constrains the state's capacity to cool down "mainland fever"—society's enthusiasm for doing business with China. In mid-1993, in an effort to stimulate exports to the United States, the Central Bank of China intervened directly in the foreign exchange market, causing a depreciation in the value of the New Taiwan dollar against the U.S. dollar.[58] However, commodity exports to the United States in 1993 still declined 6.8 percent over the year before, while indirect exports to China rose 20 percent (see Table 6.8). Policies targeted at the U.S. market did not enhance the macroeconomic situation in Taiwan as a whole.

Taiwan's economic dependence on China has put the Taiwan government in a dilemma. The state has to choose between slowing economic growth by cooling down trade relations with China and adopting more liberal cross-Straits economic policies to stimulate economic performance

TABLE 6.7   Taiwan's Trade Surplus with China and Total Trade Surplus, 1987–1995 (in US$ million)

Year	Taiwan's Trade Surplus with China	Taiwan's International Trade Surplus	%
1987	3,285.61	18,695.37	17.57%
1988	4,489.17	10,994.56	40.83%
1989	5,787.53	14,038.63	41,23%
1990	7,041.75	12,498.44	56.34%
1991	10,416.55	13,317.76	78.22%
1992	13,420.72	9,493.70	141.36%
1993	16,548.24	7,800.00	212.16%
1994	19,700.00	7,700.00	255.84%
1995	23,342.73	8,120.00	287.47%

SOURCE: *Liang'an jingji fenxi baogao* (Monthly Report on Cross-Straits Economic Relations) (Taipei, Mainland Affairs Council), June 1994, 28 and 33; *Taiwan Statistical Data Book 1993* (Taipei: Council for Economic Planning and Development, 1993), 196; Associated Press data, cited from Internet source, February 8, 1994 and January 8, 1995; Tables 6.5 and 6.6.

TABLE 6.8   Taiwan's Exports to China and the United States (in US$ million)

Year	Taiwan's Exports to China	Taiwan's Exports to the United States
1983	1,384.00	11,333.70
1984	1,764.54	14,867.70
1985	2,234.49	14,773.30
1986	2,514.23	19,013.80
1987	3,574.55	23,684.70
1988	4,967.86	23,467.10
1989	6,374.43	24,036.20
1990	7,807.11	21,745.80
1991	11,542.50	22.317.40
1992	14,539.69	23.572.10
1993	17,651.78	23,477.70
1994	20,319.00	24,345.00
1995	24,916.93	26,407.39

SOURCE: *Liang'an jingji fenxi baogao* (Monthly Report on Cross-Straits Economic Relations) (Taipei, Mainland Affairs Council), June 1994, 36; March 1995, 24 and 28; *Taiwan Statistical Data Book 1993* (Taipei: Council for Economic Planning and Development, 1993), 215; Tables 6.5 and 6.6.

at the risk of endangering national security. Furthermore, China has become a powerful competitor of Taiwan in the international market, especially with exports of nondurable consumer goods, an area in which Taiwan traditionally excelled.[60]

Taiwan has yielded to China in the export to the United States and Japan of such products as clothing and accessories, wood, bamboo products and nonmetallic furniture, and plastic products. Capital goods and durable goods have gradually become Taiwan's main export products, although China has been rapidly gaining ground in this area too over the past five years.[61]

Taiwan's general international competitiveness has also experienced a decline in the past few years. From 1983 to 1992, the New Taiwan dollar appreciated around 60 percent against the U.S. dollar.[62] Moreover, rising land and wage costs, the labor shortage, and the environmental protection movement have forced export-oriented enterprises to move offshore.

By contrast, China's exports of manufactured goods have grown consistently over the past ten years. From 1985 to 1993, the average annual growth rate was 23.9 percent.[63] A report released by Taiwan's Council for Economic Planning and Development shows that Taiwan's international competitiveness is gradually weakening compared to China in the manufacturing sector (see Table 6.9). Quantitatively, China's share of the U.S. market has surpassed that of Taiwan since 1992 (see Table 6.10).

The fact that Taiwan is heavily dependent on the China market gives the Chinese the leverage to manipulate Taiwan's domestic economy. As Kenneth Waltz argues, the word "interdependence" obscures inequalities of national capability and tricks us into believing that "all states are playing the same game." All states are definitely not playing the same game. A state that is heavily involved in the international economy and cannot shift to relative autarky is vulnerable to political leverage exercised by its trade partners.[64] Trade and commerce can become an alternative to war in relations between sovereign states. The "influence effect" of foreign trade can lead to a relationship of political dependence and influence between states.[65]

Hence, economic dependence on China has increased Taiwan's political vulnerability. From Beijing's economic policy toward Taiwan, it is obvious that the Chinese are trying to attract Taiwanese trade and investment for political reasons. In 1988, the State Council promulgated a set of twenty-two measures to encourage investment from Taiwan. These included all the special inducements offered to foreign investors in general, and some more. For example, Taiwan investors are allowed to sell stock in projects, rent government-owned factories, and take over and operate state enterprises by guaranteeing a certain amount of earnings to the state and keeping the rest. They can appoint relatives in China as agents to manage their

TABLE 6.9   The International Competitiveness of Taiwan and China in Manufacturing Sector

Type of Goods	Category	Most competitive economy	
		1986	1993
Nondurable	Food	Tie	Tie
consumer goods	Beverages & tobacco	Tie	China
	Textiles	Tie	Tie
	Apparel & accessories	Tie	Tie
	Leather, fur & products	Tie	Taiwan
	Wood, bamboo products	Taiwan	Taiwan
	Miscellaneous industrial	Tie	Tie
Durable goods	Paper products & printing	Tie	Tie
	Chemical materials	Tie	Tie
	Chemical products	China	China
	Rubber products	Tie	Tie
	Plastic products	Tie	Tie
	Nonmetalic minerals	Taiwan	China
	Basic metals	Tie	Tie
	Fabricated metal products	China	Tie
Capital goods	Machinery & equipment	Tie	Tie
	Electrical & electronic	Taiwan	Taiwan
	Transport equipment	Taiwan	Tie
	Precision instruments	Taiwan	Tie

SOURCE: *Liang'an jingmao tongxun* (Newsletter of Cross-Straits Economy) (Taipei, Straits Exchange Foundation), August 10, 1994, 13. Based on data from the Council for Economic Planning and Development, Taiwan.

TABLE 6.10   Market Shares of Taiwan and Chinese Products in the U.S. Market (in percentages)

	Taiwan Products		China Products	
Year	Market Share	Growth Rate	Market Share	Growth Rate
1986	5.37	20.7	1.29	−23.6
1987	6.12	24.4	1.55	31.9
1988	5.67	0.7	1.95	35.2
1989	5.20	−1.9	2.56	40.8
1990	4.62	−6.8	3.10	27.0
1991	4.75	1.2	3.90	23.9
1992	4.68	6.9	4.87	35.3
1993	4.35	1.80	5.47	23.2
1994	4.04	6.8	5.86	22.7

SOURCE: *Liang'an jingji fenxi baogao* (Monthly Report of Cross-Straits Economic Relations) (Taipei, Mainland Affairs Council), June 1994, 74; March 1995, 59.

projects, and there is no time limit on projects established by investors from Taiwan. Taiwanese investors can also buy and sell real estate and leave such acquired property to their heirs.[66]

That this preferential treatment is politically motivated is clear from the utterances of the Chinese leaders. For example, at the 1990 National Work Conference on Taiwan Affairs, phrases such as "promoting political integration through economic exchange," "increasing popular pressure on the government of Taiwan," and "leading to the unification of the motherland" were openly associated with cross-Straits economic relations.[67] Premier Li Peng further indicated in his "Government Report" in 1993 that the main goal of the PRC was to use economic interaction as an instrument to promote the "three links" with Taiwan, thereby achieving a breakthrough in China's unification according to the "one country, two systems" formula.[68] In brief, Taiwan's economic dependence has given China a powerful tool with which to exert political influence over the island. The special kind of "interdependence" between Taiwan and China has put Taiwan in a vulnerable situation rather than allowing it to reap the benefits of cross-Straits economic interaction.

To sum up, interdependence and neoliberal theorists hold that in the post–Cold War world, security issues no longer play the dominant role in international affairs. Domestic politics and foreign policy are closely linked, and the notion of national interest is increasingly difficult to identify. The increasing frequency of economic transactions, the rise of nonstate actors, and the decline in importance of security concerns increase the chances of cooperation among nations. Like the realists, interdependence theorists also presume that states are rational actors. They hold that economic and cultural exchanges not only promote mutual understanding but also create a network of interdependence. Nations are willing to cooperate within this network if it corresponds with their interests.

However, the presumption of rationality has its limitations. Rational action by states is constrained by two major forces: the domestic political situation and the distribution of power in the international system. Economic interdependence creates a peaceful environment for coexistence, but these two factors shape the pattern and trend of interdependence.

The domestic political and economic situation in both Taiwan and China has a major impact on cross-Straits interdependence. In Taiwan, proindependence sentiment and a desire for Taiwan-centered policies collectively force the executive branch to adopt a moderate stance toward unification. In order to win votes, the ruling KMT has had to seek a place for Taiwan in the international community as an independent political entity. Both Taipei's bid to reenter the United Nations and its hesitation about opening direct trade and communication links with China can be regarded as being for domestic consumption. On the other hand, in post-Deng China, Jiang Zemin's position is that of first among equals. He had no choice but to adopt a tough line on Taiwan in order to conciliate the military leaders. Thus, domestic political developments prevent leaders on both sides from acting in a "rational" way with respect to unification and integration. These domestic developments, plus the nationalism of the Chinese regime and Taiwan's desire for recognition, greatly influence the linkage between the "low politics" of cultural and economic cooperation and the "high politics" of unification.

Besides the domestic constraints, the asymmetry of power between the two sides of the Taiwan Straits puts Taiwan in an inferior and vulnerable situation in the process of interaction. As the preceding analysis indicates, China's strategy of political integration is in essence an attempt at political takeover through economic interaction. Economic interdependence is being utilized as a tool to achieve this ultimate goal. Hence, the functionalists' "spillover effect" is turned on its head and political motives intervene in nonpolitical issues in cross-Straits interaction. For Taiwan, the romantic dream of China's reunification has been replaced by a struggle for survival.

Conclusion

In this chapter, the utility of the "strong state paradigm" in analyzing Taiwan's policy toward economic relations with China has been challenged. The Taiwanese state lacks the capacity to regulate profit-seeking private firms by means of restrictive laws and macroeconomic policies. These firms are governed by the market mechanism in their efforts to cultivate the Chinese market, and the state can do no more than legitimize the existing situation.

The "strong state paradigm" emphasizes the ability of state leaders to resist pressure from private interests and to translate their will into public policy. The state not only provides "public goods" to society but also intervenes directly in the market system to achieve its own autonomous goals. During the 1960s and 1970s, state intervention in Taiwan was "market augmenting" in the sense that it reduced the uncertainties and risks related to business, generated and disseminated information about opportunities, and inspired the population with hope for the future.

However, the Taiwanese state's intervention in cross-Straits trade and investment in the 1990s is "market restricting." Moreover, the state lacks sufficient "vision" to guide the market. The goals of cross-Straits economic policy—market benefits or security concerns—are very ambiguous. Furthermore, as we saw in Chapter 4, state agencies lack coordination as to the pace and direction of economic relations with China.

Another factor contributing to the prevalence of market forces over the state is the dynamic attitude of Taiwan's leaders of small and medium-sized businesses. The strong state paradigm argues that it is state intervention and state incentives that have created the international competitiveness of Taiwanese firms. However, in the 1960s and 1970s, under pressure from state monopolies and big firms supported by high import tariffs, small enterprises were squeezed out of the domestic market. They had no choice but to concentrate on the international market, where they eventually accounted for more than 80 percent of Taiwan's total exports. Despite their contribution to the economy, these small firms, more than 70 percent of which were individually owned, did not qualify for major governmental assistance. According to the Regulations for Encouraging Investment, which is regarded as the most powerful tool of state intervention, only limited-liability companies can enjoy tax breaks and low-interest loans from the state.[69] Yet these mostly family enterprises absorbed surplus labor from the countryside and adopted very flexible strategies to adjust to the changing international market.

The so-called Taiwan economic miracle was created jointly by the autonomous state and dynamic small enterprises. Since the late 1980s, these small enterprises have formed the vanguard of Taiwan's assault on the Chinese market. Their business is conducted around the edges of, and sometimes in direct opposition to, Taiwan's legal restrictions. Economic benefit provides the only driving force behind their investments in China or the transfer of their labor-intensive plants to China's booming coastal provinces. Moreover, since state agencies have been slow to reach a consensus on the regulation of cross-Straits economic ties, these small firms were always one step ahead of state laws. The state has been "chasing" the market mechanism instead of "governing" it. What the state has done is to partially legitimize the existing situation rather than to act as a guide to Taiwanese businesspeople.

To sum up, given the fact that economic interaction across the Taiwan Straits has created a situation of economic dependence for Taiwan, rather than interdependence, political integration through economic cooperation, such as the creation of a "Greater China Economic Circle," seems to be a remote goal. China still treats Taiwan as a renegade province rather than an equal political partner. Cooperation on nonpolitical issues creates a peaceful environment for coexistence, but the Taiwan state's adherence to the goal of national unification is in part a response to Beijing's coercive policies rather than purely the outcome of closer interaction in nonpolitical areas. This unique situation challenges the neofunctionalist presumption that cooperation in "low politics" will lead to peace among sovereign states. For Taiwan, political survival is a more urgent issue than political integration. The real focus of conducting peace would be political elites' perception and calculation of power and hard bargaining across the Taiwan Straits. Interdependence theorists give us insights into cross-Straits interaction in the post–Cold War period, but the realists' arguments of power politics and the struggle for survival also provide a useful framework for analyzing conflicts and cooperation between the two sides of the Taiwan Straits.

Notes

1. Robert Gilpin, *The Political Economy of International Relations* (Princeton: Princeton University Press, 1987), chapter 2.

2. "Economic Policies Adjust to the Times," *Free China Review* (Taipei), January 1994, 24.

3. *Dalu gongzuo fagui huibian* (Collection of Regulations in Mainland Affairs) (Taipei: Mainland Affairs Council, 1993), v–7.

4. Data from Board of Foreign Trade, Ministry of Economic Affairs, Republic of China.

5. Kao Koong-lian, *Trade and Investment Across the Taiwan Straits* (Taipei: Mainland Affairs Council, 1993), 4.

6. Milton D. Yeh, "Ask a Tiger for Its Hide? Taiwan's Approaches to the Economic Transactions Across the Straits," (unpublished manuscript, 1994), 4.

7. Kao, *Trade and Investment*, 8.

8. *Liang'an jingmao tongxun* (Newsletter of Cross-Straits Economy) (Taipei, Straits Exchange Foundation) , March 1993, 7.

9. *Gongshang shibao* (Commercial Times) (Taipei), January 26, 1994.

10. *Dow Jones International News*, March 7, 1993. Cited from Internet resource of *China News Digest*.

11. *Ziyou shibao* (Liberty Times) (Taipei), December 12, 1993.

12. *Minzhong ribao* (Popular News) (Taipei), June 25, 1994.

13. Kao, *Trade and Investment*, 5.

14. *Liang'an jingji nianbao* (Annual Report on Cross-Straits Economy) (Taipei: Chung-Hua Institution for Economic Research, 1994), 236.

15. Kao Charng, "Economic Interactions Between Two Sides of the Taiwan Straits," in *Conference on the Evolution of Taiwan Within a New World Economic Order* (Taipei: Chung-Hua Institution for Economic Research, 1993), 339.

16. *Lianhe bao* (United Daily News) (Taipei), December 31, 1995.

17. *Free China Review* 44, no. 1 (1994):10.

18. *Lianhe bao*, December 31, 1995.

19. Liu An-kuo, a Taiwanese lamp maker with investment projects in China, interview with the author, August 1, 1994.

20. Ibid.

21. Kao Hsi-chun and Li Cheng, *Taiwan tupo liang'an jingmao zhuizong* (Tracing the Cross-Straits Economy) (Taipei: Commonwealth Publishing, 1992), 196.

22. Ho Yung-ching et al., *Touzi dalu shichang* (Investing in the Mainland Market) (Taipei: Management Science Association, 1993), 42.

23. *Lianhe bao*, December 31, 1995.

24. *Collected Regulations of Investing on Mainland China* (Taipei: Ministry of Economic Affairs, 1993).

25. *Lianhe bao*, October 12, 1993.

26. *Shijie ribao* (World Journal News) (New York), March 28, 1994.

27. Shea Jia-dong and Yang Ya-hwei, "Taiwan's Financial System and the Allocation of Investment Funds," in *The Role of the State in Taiwan's Development*, ed. Joel Aberbach, David Dollar, and Kenneth Sokoloff (New York: M. E. Sharpe, 1994), 193–230.

28. *Gongshang shibao*, June 11, 1993.

29. *Zhongshi zhoukan* (China Times Weekly), September 18, 1993, 19.

30. Ho, *Touzi dalu shichang*, 38.

31. Yang Ya-hui, "Taiwan's Monetary Policies and Economic Development," in *Industrial Development and Economic Policy* (Taipei: Chung-Hua Institute for Economic Research, 1993), 198.

32. Yeh, "Ask a Tiger for Its Hide?" 6.

33. *Gongshang shibao*, May 15, 1993.

34. Chen An and Peng Li, "An Analysis of the Agreement to Protect Taiwanese Investments in the Mainland," *Taiwan yanjiu* (Taiwan Studies) (Xiamen), no. 4 (1993):60.

35. Working document of Straits Exchange Foundation.

36. Chen Jung-yuan and Chang Kuo-pao, staff members of Straits Exchange Foundation, interview with the author, August 10, 1994.

37. Liu An-kuo interview.

38. Unpublished manuscript by Tai-Yu Management Consultants, Taipei, Taiwan.

39. *Gongshang shibao*, April 12, 1995.

40. Chen Jung-yuan interview.

41. Wu Yu-shan, "Mainland China's Economic Policy Toward Taiwan: Economic Reform vs. Unification" (paper delivered at the twenty-third Sino-American Conference, Taipei, Taiwan, June 6–9, 1994), 19.

42. Tzong-biau Lin, "Golden Growth Triangle and Economic Integration in the Southern Part of China" (paper presented at the 22nd Sino-American Conference on Contemporary China, Washington, D.C., June 22, 1993), 9.

43. *Zhongguo shibao* (China Times) (Taipei), July 27, 1995.

44. *Liang'an jingji tongji yuebao* (Monthly Statistics on Cross-Straits Economy) (Taipei, Mainland Affairs Council, September 1995), 58.

45. Robert Ash and Y. Kueh, "Trade and Investment Flows Between China, Hong Kong, and Taiwan," *China Quarterly* 136 (December 1993):721–722. For economic complementarity within Greater China, see James Myers and Donald Puchala, "Greater China: Some American Reflections," *Asian Affairs* 21, no. 1 (Spring 1994); Murray Weidenbaum, "Greater China," *Vital Speeches*, December 1, 1993; "The Rise of Greater China," *Current*, December 1993.

46. Edmund Dell, *Politics of Economic Interdependence* (New York: St. Martin's Press, 1987).

47. Kym Anderson and Richard Blackhurst, *Regional Integration and the Global Trading System* (New York: Harvester, 1993), 7.

48. Cheng Chu-yuan, "Toward the Formation of a Greater China Economic Sphere" (paper presented at the 36th Annual Meeting of the American Association of Chinese Studies, San Antonio, November 11, 1994).

49. *Japan Economic Newswire*, April 4, 1994. Internet resource.

50. James Hsiung, "Cross-Straits Economic Cooperation and the 21st Century World" (paper delivered at the Third Cross-Straits Relations Conference, Ningbo, China, August 2–6, 1993), 4.

51. *Jingji ribao* (Economic Daily) (Taipei), July 1, 1993.

52. A. F. K. Organski, *World Politics* (New York: Knopf, 1958).

53. Peter Robson, *The Economics of International Integration* (London: George Allen and Unwin, 1984), 151, 169.

54. For the functionalist view of interdependence, see Ernst Hass, *The Uniting of Europe* (Stanford: Stanford University Press, 1957); David Mitrany, *A Working Peace System* (Chicago: Quadrangle, 1966); Robert Keohane and Joseph Nye, *Power and Interdependence* (Boston: Little Brown, 1977).

55. Steve Chan, "Peace by Pieces? Mainland-Taiwan Transaction Flows" (paper presented at the annual meeting of the American Political Science Association, New York, September 1–4, 1994).

56. John Garnett, "States, State-Centric Perspective, and Interdependence Theory," in *Dilemmas of World Politics*, ed. John Baylis and N. J. Rengger (Oxford: Clarendon Press, 1992), 74–75.

57. Charng Kao and Tzung-Ta Yen, *A Study on the Economic Relations between Taiwan and Mainland China* (Taipei: Chung-Hua Institution for Economic Research, 1992), tables 2 and 3.

58. *Lianhe bao*, May 22, 1993.

59. *Liang'an jingji fenxi baogao* (Monthly Report on Cross-Straits Economic Relations) (Taipei, Mainland Affairs Council, June 1994), 74.

60. "Durable goods" includes paper products, chemical materials, rubber products, nonmetallic minerals, basic metals, fabricated metal products, etc.; "nondurable goods" include food, beverages, textiles, apparel, leather, fur, wood, etc.; "capital goods" include machinery, equipment, electrical machinery, transportation equipment, and precision instruments.

61. Kao, "Economic Interactions Between Two Sides," 357.

62. Calculated from *The Republic of China Yearbook 1993* (Taipei: Government Information Office, 1993), 239.

63. Nicholas Lardy, *China in the World Economy* (Washington, D.C.: Institute of International Economics, 1994), 31.

64. Kenneth Waltz, "The Myth of National Interdependence," in *The International Cooperation*, ed. Charles Kindleberger (Cambridge: MIT Press, 1970), 205–223.

65. Albert Hirschman, *National Power and the Structure of Foreign Trade* (Berkeley: University of California Press, 1969), 15.

66. *Foreign Broadcast Information Service—China*, March 29, 1989, 72; Ralph Clough, *Reaching Across the Taiwan Strait* (Boulder: Westview Press, 1993), 42.

67. Yen Tzung-ta, "Retrospection and Reflection on the Impact of Cross-Strait Economic Relations," in *Liang'an guanxi yu Zhongguo qiantu xueshu yantaohui Lunwenji* (Proceedings of Cross-Straits Relations, and the Future of China) (Taipei: Democracy Foundation, 1991), 59.

68. Chen Teh-sheng, *Liang'an zhengjing hudong* (Political-Economic Interaction across the Taiwan Straits) (Taipei: Yung-yeh, 1994), 58. The "three links" refers to direct trade, direct postal service, and direct transportation.

69. Kao Hsichun and Li Cheng, eds., *Taiwan jingyan sishinian* (Forty Years of Taiwan Experience) (Taipei: Commonwealth, 1991), 338–378.

7

Conclusion

This book begins with a central question: What has been the impact of democratization on state-society relations and cross-Straits economic policy in Taiwan? The previous six chapters have dealt with the process of democratization, divisions within the state, the rise of social interests, and the importance of the market mechanism in the policymaking process. The purpose of this concluding chapter is, first of all, to review the findings and to provide an overall picture of the failure of state intervention in cross-Straits economic policy. Second, an attempt will be made to identify the insights this case study can provide into Taiwan's political economy and state-society relations in general in the era of democratization.

Reasons for the Failure of State Intervention in Cross-Straits Economic Relations

Impact of Democratization

Democratization has changed the structure of the state and state-society relations in Taiwan. In the authoritarian era, major policies reflected the will of the supreme leaders, first Chiang Kai-shek and then his son, Chiang Ching-kuo. Politicians of the ruling Kuomintang maintained a patron-client relationship with the technocrats responsible for substantial economic planning. The state elite was a coherent body. Major social forces, including peasants, labor, and the opposition, exerted only minimal constraints on state policymaking capacity.

The state's domination over society has diminished since the beginning of the democratization process. As discussed in Chapter 2, Taiwan's democratization is neither a top-down nor a bottom-up revolution. No single force has played a decisive role in the process, and the consequence has proved to be cooperation between the state and society. The state elite is divided on the content, tempo, and strategies of democratization, and as democratization has progressed, different social interests, represented by competing factions within the state and opposition parties, have begun to demand more political power and to participate directly in the political process. To initiate policies, the state has to compromise with factional interests and satisfy various social demands at the same time.

However, the capacity of the state to institutionalize social interests and to create a new set of rules for political competition has proved to be inadequate. Dialogue has been established between the ruling party and opposition forces, but a smooth process of conciliation and consensus building is lacking. Riven by factional conflicts itself, the KMT has found it more and more difficult to accommodate social demands. Social groups, therefore, have resorted to channels outside state institutions to express their discontent. Hence, although the state has strict regulations concerning political and social activities such as demonstrations and election campaigns, very few people respect the law.

This lack of respect for the law is just one side effect of democratization. Social forces have been released, but institutionalization lags behind society's demands. In cross-Straits economic relations, this is reflected in the business community's determination to enter the booming China market in the face of state prohibition. This disdain for the state's power to use the law as an instrument of coercion has created a new political culture of distrust for public authority. This is an important reason for the social disorder that has occurred during the process of democratic transition and the failure of legal restrictions on cross-Straits economic interaction.

Lack of Bureaucratic Coordination

The bureaucratic policymaking process is full of contradictions and conflicts. After the establishment of several supraministerial bodies, the dominant player in the China policy bureaucracy is still the Mainland Affairs Council, which has grasped more power on the pretext of "coordinating" policy.

However, bureaucratic conflicts have not been reduced as a result of the concentration of power in the hands of the MAC. In particular, the MAC and the Ministry of Economic Affairs have clashed over some important issues, such as the opening of direct trade and direct transportation links with China. Whereas the MAC has argued that political concerns should take precedence over the market mechanism, the MOEA's policy proposals have been based on cost-benefit analysis and reflect the interests of the business community. Conflicts between the MAC and the semiofficial Straits Exchange Foundation have also been fierce. Personality differences and divergent perceptions of the power and autonomy of the SEF are the main factors here. Policymaking with regard to Taiwan-China economic relations has become a continuous process of pulling and hauling between conflicting branches of the bureaucracy. The direct results of this interagency infighting are slow response to social demands and contradictory policy directives.

Fair rules of the political game have yet to be established in Taiwan's China policy bureaucracy. Dissident opinions are sometimes neglected or suppressed in the policymaking process. In some cases, as discussed in Chapter 4, the "dissident party," usually the MOEA, has appealed directly to the public to relieve its dissatisfaction at the arbitrary behavior of the MAC. The MOEA has released trial balloons to test society's reaction to its proposals and attempted to add to its bargaining power by forging alliances with private business to push for changes in state policies. The introduction of exterior forces has turned policymaking into a prolonged process of confrontation between social interests and political considerations.

Institutional conflicts are in part a reflection of political and social contradictions in Taiwan. Factional politics and the conflict between politicians from the mainstream and nonmainstream factions of the KMT are involved in the MAC-SEF confrontation. The subethnic factor, whose resurgence is an unexpected outcome of liberalization, has not only impeded positive action promoted by the mainlander elite but has also influenced power distribution and elite recruitment. Moreover, as discussed in Chapter 3, the KMT party-state has had to accommodate rising demand for Taiwan independence inside and outside the state hierarchy. Since closer economic interaction with China could be regarded as promoting "hasty unification," the state has adopted a more conservative policy of indirect trade and investment under the banner of protecting national security. This policy is not based on a rational calculation of costs and benefits but is the outcome of political compromise.

Penetration of Business Interests

Big business groups began their advance into the booming China market in 1991. In contrast to the export-oriented small enterprises that blazed the trail of cross-Straits economic transactions, big business groups are forming joint ventures with Chinese firms and multinational corporations. Their investment projects are aimed at the domestic market in China, rather than the export market, and form part of the companies' overall globalization plans. But in addition to its own interests, big business is being pushed into the China market by its customers, the smaller scale "downstream" industries that have already transferred their factories across the Straits.

Taiwanese big business has developed political networks on both sides of the Straits to protect its interests in China. Through personal connections (*guanxi*) and a variety of alliances with the state and the KMT, enterprise groups are able to influence the policymaking process. Through business organizations such as the Chinese National Federation of Industries and the Chinese National Association of Industry and Commerce, business leaders urge the government to lift the ban on direct trade and investment in China. Big business also exerts its influence on the legislature. Through the receipt of campaign contributions, many legislators become the representatives of local factions and business interests. The business-legislature linkage is now closer than it was before. Individual legislators are not concerned with initiating new policies but with protecting the interests of their business patrons in the course of the development and implementation of China policy. They play the role of "brokers" in promoting and protecting Taiwanese business interests in China, and the state has to persuade and bargain with the legislature and individual legislators in order to get major economic policies passed.

The case of Y. C. Wang's Formosa Group, which is discussed in Chapter 5, provides a good example of state-business conflict and cooperation. Investment projects in China have in general proved useful to big business in its bargaining with the state. The ultimate goal of these firms is domestic economic benefits, and a pending project in China serves as a tool to achieve this goal. In Wang's case, financial strength gave him sufficient autonomy to manipulate the governments on both sides of the Taiwan Straits. Wang finally established his project in Taiwan, but his ambitions with regard to the China market have not diminished. Although the state may prevail in individual cases, it lacks the long-term vision necessary for governing private interests.

Challenge from the Market Mechanism

Out of concern for national security and economic development, Taiwan has adopted a mercantilist policy of economic regulation. Economic nationalism of the mercantilist variety emphasizes the political framework of economic activities and recognizes that markets must function in a world of competitive groups and states. Hence, the Taiwanese state tries to intervene directly in cross-Straits economic interaction, utilizing coercive political instruments to deter Taiwanese from doing business with China directly.

However, as the analysis in Chapter 6 indicates, the regulative policies of the state have failed to halt the stampede into the China market. A large portion of economic transactions are conducted directly in defiance of the government's ban. The huge statistical gap between official data and actual values of trade and investment demonstrates that the state's capacity in this area is weak. Taiwanese businesspeople adopt very flexible strategies to resist state intervention and to operate outside state control. Neither financial instruments nor business regulations have a major impact on their daily operations. What really controls their activities are the economic benefits to be gained from the booming China market.

Although the state has tried hard to cool down the "mainland fever," Taiwan's economic development has become more and more dependent on the China market. Indeed, without its exports to China, Taiwan would have registered a trade deficit since 1993. Now, the state is forced to choose between slowing down economic growth by restricting trade relations with China or adopting more liberal policies to stimulate economic performance at the risk of endangering national security. But economic dependence not only limits the state's capacity to intervene effectively in economic transactions but also gives China leverage to manipulate Taiwan's domestic economy for political ends. The asymmetry of political and economic power between the two sides of the Taiwan Straits also acts as an impediment to political unification through economic integration of the "Great China Economic Circle," as discussed in Chapter 6.

In brief, the main reason for the state's failure to enforce its regulations with regard to business links with China is that it lacks a long-term economic development plan. In contrast to the "market augmenting" policy of the economic takeoff period, the Taiwanese state's policy toward cross-Straits economic transactions is "market restricting." The state's failure to enforce its restrictions on cross-Straits economic relations is due to a combination of poor political and bureaucratic coordination within the state and the ascendance of dynamic social interests. The balance of power between the state and society has changed. Democratization has reduced state autonomy and state capacity and also created a new form of state-society interaction.

State and Society in Taiwan Revisited

This study challenges the utility of the "strong-state paradigm" in explaining Taiwan's political economy in the era of democratization. The strong-state paradigm characterizes economic success as being the result of autonomous policies initiated by a political-bureaucratic elite insulated from social pressure. This kind of state understands the need for methods of economic intervention that are based on the price mechanism. An authoritarian political system provides the necessary insulation for the state and enhances its intervention capacity.

Authority in the developmental state does not come from Weber's "holy trinity" of traditional, rational-legal, and charismatic sources. It is, rather, the authority of a people committed to the transformation of their social, political, and economic order. Legitimation results from the state's achievements, not from the way it came to power.[1] During Taiwan's authoritarian years, the legitimacy of the KMT party-state was based on economic growth and a fairly equal distribution of income. The ultimate national goal was to survive and prosper in spite of military threats from the other side of the Taiwan Straits. The myth of recovering the mainland mobilized the whole population toward a single goal of national development.

As the myth of recovering mainland China gradually lost its attraction, the KMT party-state began to transform itself into an indigenous Taiwanese regime. Since the KMT decided to open the regime to democratic competition, the legitimacy of the state has been based on the consent of the people. To win elections, the ruling party has to incorporate dissident opinions and different policy proposals for national development. This gives civil society, especially the strong middle class, plenty of opportunity to penetrate the state hierarchy. In contrast to the achievement-oriented strong state of the authoritarian era, the Taiwanese state of the democratization era lacks a common goal that it shares with society. Besides economic development, the state has to satisfy the various goals of society, such as political participation and social justice. State policies must be based on social demands that are the sources of the regime's legitimacy. Policy outcomes are the result of a collective endeavor involving state and society.

Another characteristic of the strong state is a coherent political elite in charge of economic planning. There were certainly political struggles in the higher echelons of the state hierarchy during the authoritarian era in Taiwan, but technocrats managed to maintain their insulation from political influence and social pressure. This has changed since the democratization process began. As soon as the supreme leader Chiang Ching-kuo passed from the scene, the KMT was riven by a struggle for power. The party divided into two main factions, and as a result, all aspects of national affairs became politicized. Technocrats were classified according to factional affiliations, and new patron-client relationships developed along factional lines. Moreover, because of his own background as an economic technocrat, President Lee Teng-hui himself intervened actively in the substantial policymaking process. This has led to a congruence, rather than a separation, of political interests and economic policymaking power. The power struggle at the highest level has penetrated the cross-Straits policymaking process.

Social interests, especially business interests, play a more important role since democratization began. As the pressure to win elections has increased, the ruling party has developed various alliances with business groups from which it obtains campaign funds. Through political donations, business associations, and alliances with KMT enterprises, business groups have worked to obtain political protection for their economic interests. The allocation of political resources is no longer decided by autonomous edict issued by the political elite but through a process of conciliation and cooperation between the state and business.

Social interests also use the legislature and opposition parties as channels to influence policymaking. During the authoritarian era, the legislative branch and the opposition exerted only minimal constraint on the executive. But since the first comprehensive election of the Legislative Yuan in 1992, the legislature has served as a link between social interests and the state. Members of local factions and domestic capitalists have become active participants in the legislature. Moreover, the most powerful opposition party, the Democratic Progressive Party, has attracted more and more voters from Taiwan's energetic middle class. To realize its policies, the state has had to establish formal and informal channels of communication with the legislative branch and opposition forces.

In conclusion, this case study of Taiwan's cross-Straits economic policy shows that the capacity and autonomy of the Taiwanese state have diminished greatly since democratization. In the 1960s and 1970s, the strong state prevailed over society and achieved Taiwan's economic miracle. Since then, democratization and economic development have created a strong middle class and new actors in the political game, including the opposition parties, domestic capitalists, and profit-seeking entrepreneurs, as well as the bureaucracy itself, which has been divided by factional struggles. The state has begun to develop a relationship of coexistence with society. The agenda for research into Taiwan's political economy in the democratization era must incorporate these new actors in society and bureaucratic conflicts.

Democracy and economic efficiency are not absolutely mutually exclusive, but the existence of a dynamic society and the need to accommodate do weaken the state's policymaking capacity. The Taiwanese state is not exactly "weak," but the degree of institutionalization of state-society interaction is inadequate. Future research should deal with the continuous process of state-society bargaining and the increasing importance of such representatives of social interests as the legislature and business associations. Only by studying this state-society interaction can the changing nature of the Taiwanese state during its political and economic transition be fully understood.

Notes

1. Chalmers Johnson, "The Developmental State: Odyssey of a Concept" (unpublished manuscript, 1995).

Selected Bibliography

Aberbach, Joel, David Dollar, and Kenneth Sokoloff, eds. *The Role of the State in Taiwan's Development*. New York: M. E. Sharpe, 1994.

Alardt, Frik, ed., *Mass Politics: Studies in Political Society*. New York: Free Press, 1970.

Allison, Graham T, *Essence of Decision: Explaining the Cuban Missile Crisis*. Boston: Little Brown, 1971.

Amsden, Alice. *Asia's Next Giant: South Korea and Late Industrialization*. Oxford: Oxford University Press, 1989.

Anderson, Kym, and Richard Blackhurst. *Regional Integration and the Global Trading System*. New York: Harvester, 1993.

Ash, Robert, and Y. Kueh. "Trade and Investment Flows Between China, Hong Kong, and Taiwan." *China Quarterly*, no. 136 (December 1993).

Bau, Tzong-ho. "The Essence of Beijing's Policy Toward Taiwan." Paper presented at the annual meeting of the American Political Science Association, September 2–5, 1993.

Baylis, John, and N. J. Rengger, eds. *Dilemmas of World Politics*. Oxford: Clarendon Press, 1992.

Berger, Peter, and Hsin-huang Hsiao, eds., *In Search of an East Asian Development Model*. New Brunswick: Transaction Books, 1988.

Bowles, Samuel, and Herbert Gintis. *Democracy and Capitalism*. New York: Basic Books, 1987.

Brass, Paul. *Ethnic Groups and the State*. Totowa, N.J.: Barnes and Noble, 1985.

Caituan faren haixia jiaoliu jijinhui 83 nian nianbao (Annual Report of Straits Exchange Foundation 1993). Taipei: Straits Exchange Foundation, 1994.

Caporaso, James, and David Levine. *Theories of Political Economy*. Cambridge: Cambridge University Press, 1992.

Chan, Steve. *East Asian Dynamism*. Boulder: Westview Press, 1990.

_____. "Peace by Pieces? Mainland-Taiwan Transaction Flows." Paper presented at the annual meeting of the American Political Science Association, New York, September 1–4, 1994.

Chang, Chun-hung. *Dao zhizheng zhi lu: Difang baowei zhongyang zhi li lun yu shiji* (The Road to Power—Theory and Practice of Encircling the Center from the Periphery). Taipei: Nan Fang, 1989.

Chao, Chi-chang. *Meiyuande yunyong* (Using American Aid). Taipei: Linking, 1985.

Chen, An, and Li Peng. "An Analysis of the Agreement to Protect Taiwanese Investments in the Mainland." *Taiwan yanjiu* (Taiwan Studies), no. 4 (Xiamen) (1993).

Chen, Chung-hsin. "DPP's Mainland Policy and Cross-Straits Relations." Paper presented at the Conference on Cross-Straits Relations, sponsored by the Chinese University of Hong Kong, Hong Kong, July 1992.

Chen, Shih-meng, et al. *Jiege dangguo zibenzhuyi* (Deconstructing Party-State Capitalism). Taipei: Cheng-she, 1991.

Chen, Teh-sheng. *Liang'an zhengjing hudong* (Political-Economic Interaction Across the Taiwan Straits). Taipei: Yung-yeh, 1994.

Cheng, Chu-yuan. "Toward the Formation of a Greater China Economic Sphere." Paper presented at the 36th annual meeting of the American Association of Chinese Studies, San Antonio, November 11, 1994.

Cheng, Tun-jen, and Stephan Haggard, eds. *Political Changes in Taiwan.* Boulder: Lynne Rienner, 1992.

Cheng, Tun-jen, Chi Huang, and Samuel S. G. Wu, eds. *Inherited Rivalry: Conflict Across the Taiwan Straits.* Boulder: Lynne Rienner, 1995.

Chiu, Hungdah. "Constitutional Development and Reform in the Republic of China in Taiwan." *Issues & Studies* 29, no. 1 (January 1993):24.

_____. "Koo-Wang Talks and the Prospect of Building Constructive and Stable Relations Across the Taiwan Straits." Paper presented at the Sino-American Conference on Contemporary China, Washington, D.C., June 20–22, 1993.

Chiu, Hungdah, ed. *China and the Question of Taiwan: Documents and Analysis.* New York: Praeger, 1973.

Chiu, Hungdah, and Shao-chuan Leng, eds. *China: Seventy Years After the 1911 Hsin-Hai Revolution.* Charlottesville: University Press of Virginia, 1984.

Chou, Yu-jen. *Zhengzhi yu jingjizhi guanxi* (The Relationship between Politics and the Economy). Taipei: Wu-nan, 1993.

Chou, Yu-kou. *Li denghui diyi qiantian* (The First Thousand Days of Lee Teng-hui). Taipei: Mai Tien, 1993.

Chu, Yun-han. *Crafting Democracy in Taiwan.* Taipei: Institute for National Policy Research, 1992.

Conference on the Evolution of Taiwan Within a New World Economic Order. Taipei: Chung-Hua Institution for Economic Research, 1993.

Dahl, Robert. *Democracy and Its Critics.* New Haven: Yale University Press, 1989.

Dalu gongzuo fagui huibian (Collection of Regulations on Mainland Affairs Work). Taipei: Mainland Affairs Council, 1993.

Dell, Edmund. *Politics of Economic Interdependence.* New York: St. Martin's Press, 1987.

Deyo, Fred. *Beneath the Miracle: Labor Subordination in the New Asian Industrialism.* Berkeley: University of California Press, 1989.

Diamond, Larry, Seymour Martin Lipset, and Juan Linz. "Building and Sustaining Democratic Government in Developing Countries." *World Affairs* 150, no. 1 (Summer 1987): 5–19.

Disanjie haixia liangan guanxi yantaohui lunwen (Proceedings of the Third Annual Meeting on Cross-Straits Relations). Ningbo, China: 1993.

Domes, Jurgen. "Taiwan in 1992." *Asian Survey* 33, no. 1 (January 1993).

Fatton, Robert. *Predatory Rule: State and Civil Society in Africa.* Boulder: Lynne Rienner, 1992.

Friedman, David. *The Misunderstood Miracle*. Ithaca: Cornell University Press, 1988.

Gereffi, Gary, and Donald Wyman, eds. *Manufacturing Miracles*. Princeton: Princeton University Press, 1990.

Gilpin, Robert. *The Political Economy of International Relations*. Princeton: Princeton University Press, 1987.

Gold, Thomas. *State and Society in the Taiwan Miracle*. New York: M. E. Sharpe, 1986.

Gramsci, Antonio. *Selections from the Prison Notebooks*. Edited by Quintin Hoare and Geoffrey Smith. New York: International Publishers, 1971.

Guojia tongyi gangling (Guidelines for National Unification) (Taipei: Government Information Office, 1991).

Haggard, Stephan. *Pacific Dynamics: The International Politics of Industrial Change*. Boulder: Westview Press, 1989.

_____. *Pathways From the Periphery*. Ithaca: Cornell University Press, 1990.

Harding, Harry. "The Concept of 'Greater China': Themes, Variations, and Reservations." *China Quarterly*, no. 136 (December 1993):660–687.

Hass, Ernst. *The Uniting of Europe*. Stanford: Stanford University Press, 1957.

Hirschman, Albert. *National Power and the Structure of Foreign Trade*. Berkeley: University of California Press, 1969.

Ho, Yung-ching, et al. *Touzi dalu shichang* (Investing in the Mainland Market). Taipei: Management Science Association, 1993.

Hsia, Chi-yueh. "The Use of American Aid Over the Past Ten Years." *Caizheng jingji yuekan* (Journal of Finance and Economy), no. 12 (Taipei) (1959).

Hsiao, Hsin-huang. *Government Agricultural Policies in Taiwan and South Korea*. Taipei: Academia Sinica, 1981.

Hsiung, James. "Cross-Straits Economic Cooperation and the 21st Century World." Paper delivered at the Third Cross-Straits Relations Conference, Ningbo, China, August 2–6, 1993.

Hsu, Jui-shih. *Zhengshang guanxi jiedu* (An Analysis of State-Business Relations). Taipei: Yuan-liu, 1991.

Hu, Jason, ed. *Quiet Revolution*. Taipei: Government Information Office, 1994.

Huang, Ching-hsin. *Banshijide fendou: Wu Huoshi xiansheng koushu zhu-anji* (Business as a Vocation: The Autobiography of Mr. Wu Ho-su). Taipei: Yuncheng, 1990.

Huang, Kun-huei. "Report of the Mainland Affairs Council to the Legislative Yuan." Unpublished handout, Mainland Affairs Council, Taiwan, October 1993.

Huang, Teh-fu. "Modernization, Electoral Competition, and Local Factions in Taiwan." Paper delivered at the annual meeting of the American Political Science Association, Washington, D.C., 1993.

_____. *Minzhu jinbudang yu taiwan diqu zhengzhi minzhuhua* (The Democratic Progressive Party and Taiwan's Democratization). Taipei: Shih Ying, 1992.

Huang, Tien-chung, and Wu-yueh Chang, eds. *Liang'an guanxi yu dalu zhengce* (Cross-Straits Relations and Mainland Policy). Taipei: Wu Nan, 1993.

Huntington, Samuel. *Political Order in Changing Societies*. New Haven: Yale University Press, 1968.

_____. The Third Wave: Democratization in the Late Twentieth Century. Norman: University of Oklahoma Press, 1991.

_____. "Will More Countries Become Democratic," Political Science Quarterly 99, no. 2 (Summer 1984):193–218.

Ikenberry, G. John, ed. American Foreign Policy: Theoretical Essays (Boston: Scott, Foresman, and Company, 1989).

Ikenberry, John, David Lake, and Michael Mastanduno. The State and American Foreign Economic Policy. Ithaca: Cornell University Press, 1988.

Inoguchi, Takashi, and Daniel Okimoto, eds. The Political Economy of Japan. Stanford: Stanford University Press, 1988.

Introduction to the Republic of China's Organization for the Handling of Mainland Affairs. Taipei: Mainland Affairs Council, 1994.

Ishida, Takeshi, and Ellis S. Krauss, eds. Democracy in Japan. Pittsburgh: Pittsburgh University Press, 1989.

Jacoby, Neil H. U.S. Aid to Taiwan. New York: Praeger, 1966.

Johnson, Chalmers. MITI and the Japanese Miracle. Stanford: Stanford University Press, 1982.

Kang, Lu-tao. Li Guoding koushu lishi (An Oral History of Li Kwoh-ting). Taipei: Chuo-yueh, 1993.

Kao, Charng, and Tzung-Ta Yen. A Study on the Economic Relations Between Taiwan and Mainland China. Taipei: Chung-Hua Institution for Economic Research, 1992.

Kao, Hsi-chun, and Cheng Li. Taiwan tupo liang'an jingmao zhuizong (Tracing the Cross-Straits Economy). Taipei: Commonwealth Publishing, 1992.

Kao, Hsi-chun, and Cheng Li, eds. Taiwan jingyan sishinian (Forty Years of Taiwan Experience). Taipei: Commonwealth, 1991.

Kao, Koong-lian. Trade and Investment Across the Taiwan Straits. Taipei: Mainland Affairs Council, 1993.

Katzenstein, Peter, ed. Between Power and Plenty. Madison: University of Wisconsin Press, 1978.

_____. Small States in World Markets. Ithaca: Cornell University Press, 1986.

Keane, John. Democracy and Civil Society. London: Verso Press, 1988.

Keohane, Robert, and Joseph Nye. Power and Interdependence. Boston: Little Brown, 1977.

Kindleberger, Charles, ed. The International Cooperation. Cambridge: MIT Press, 1970.

Kitschelt, Herbert. "Political Regime Change: Structure and Process-Driven Explanations." American Political Science Review 186, no. 4 (December 1992):1028–1035.

Krasner, Stephen. "Approaches to the State: Alternative Conceptions and Historical Dynamics." Comparative Politics 16, no. 2 (January 1984).

_____. Defending the National Interest. Princeton: Princeton University Press, 1987.

Kuan, John. "KMT-CCP Negotiations and China's Unification." Paper presented at the annual meeting of the American Political Science Association, Washington, D.C., August 29–September 1, 1991.

Kuo, Cheng-tian. Global Competitiveness and Industrial Growth in Taiwan and the Philippines. Pittsburgh: University of Pittsburgh Press, 1995.

Kuo, Li-ming, ed. *Zhonggong duitai zhengce ziliao xuanji, 1949–1991* (Mainland China's Policy Toward Taiwan: Selected Documents, 1949–1991). Taipei: Yungyeh, 1992.

Lai, Tse-han, Wou Wei, and Ramon Myers. *A Tragic Beginning.* Stanford: Stanford University Press, 1992.

Lardy, Nicholas. *China in the World Economy.* Washington, D.C.: Institute of International Economics, 1994.

Lee, Kuen. *New East Asian Economic Development.* New York: M. E. Sharpe, 1993.

Lee, Kuo-hsiung. "The Politics of ROC's Constitutional Reform." Paper presented at the 36th annual meeting of APSA, Washington D.C., September 2–5, 1993.

Lee, Teng-hui. "Inaugural Address of the Eighth-Term President." In *Creating the Future.* Taipei: Government Information Office, 1992.

_____. *Speech to the Commencement Ceremony of National Chengchi University.* Taipei: Presidential Office, June 12, 1993.

Leng, Shao-chuan, ed. *Chiang Ching-kuo's Leadership in the Development of the Republic of China on Taiwan.* Lanham, Maryland: University Press of America, 1993.

Leng, Shao-chuan, and Cheng-yi Lin. "Political Change on Taiwan: Transition to Democracy?" *China Quarterly,* no. 136 (December 1993):813.

Leng, Tse-Kang. "State, Business, and Economic Interaction Across the Taiwan Strait." *Issues and Studies* 31, no. 11 (November 1995):40–59.

_____. "Taiwan-China Relations in the 1990s: Toward Economic Integration?" *Southeast Review of Asian Studies* 17 (December 1995):55–68.

Li, Cheng, and Lynn White. "Elite Transformation and Modern Change in Mainland China and Taiwan: Empirical Data and the Theory of Technocracy." *China Quarterly* (March 1990):1–35.

Liang'an guanxi yu Zhongguo qiantu xueshu yantaohui Lunwenji (Proceedings of Cross-Straits Relations and the Future of China). Taipei: Democracy Foundation, 1991.

Liang'an jingji nianbao (Annual Report on Cross-Straits Economy). Taipei: Chung-Hua Institution for Economic Research, 1994.

Liang'an jingji tongji yuebao (Monthly Statistics on Cross-Straits Economy) various issues (Taipei, Mainland Affairs Council).

Liang'an zhihangde wenti yu zhanwang (Problems and Prospect of Cross-Straits Direct Transportation). Taipei: Mainland Affairs Council, 1994.

Lieberthal, Kenneth, and Michael Oksenberg. *Policy Making in China.* Princeton: Princeton University Press, 1988.

Lin, Chong-pin. "Beijing and Taiwan: Interaction in the Post-Tiananmen Period." *China Quarterly,* no.136 (December 1993):770–805.

Lin, Tzong-biau. "Golden Growth Triangle and Economic Integration in the Southern Part of China." Paper presented at the 22nd Sino-American Conference on Contemporary China, Washington, D.C., June 22, 1993.

Lindblom, Charles. *Democracy and Market System.* Oslo: Norwegian University Press, 1988.

Linz, Juan. "Transitions to Democracy." *Washington Quarterly* 13, no. 3 (Summer 1990):143–164.

March, James, and Johan Olsen. *Rediscovering Institutions.* New York: The Free Press, 1989.

The Meaning of One China. Taipei: Mainland Affairs Council, August 1992.

Mezey, Michael. *Comparative Legislatures.* Durham: Duke University Press, 1979.

Minzhu jinbudang dalu zhengce jiben wenjian (Basic Documents of the DPP's Mainland Policy). Unpublished manuscript, 1994.

Minzhu jinbudang zhengce baipishu (Policy White Paper of the Democratic Progressive Party). Taipei: DPP Headquarters, August 1993.

Mitrany, David. *A Working Peace System.* Chicago: Quadrangle, 1966.

Moore, Barrington. *The Social Origins of Dictatorship and Democracy.* Harmondsworth, England: Penguin, 1966.

Myers, James, and Donald Puchala. "Greater China: Some American Reflections." *Asian Affairs* 21, no. 1 (Spring 1994).

Myers, Ramon, ed. *A Unique Relationship.* Stanford: Stanford University Press, 1989.

Nathan, Andrew J. "The Legislative Yuan Elections in Taiwan: Consequences of the Electoral System." *Asian Survey* 23, no. 4 (April 1993).

O'Donnell, Guillermo. *Bureaucratic-Authoritarianism: Argentina, 1966–1973, in Comparative Perspective.* Berkeley: University of California Press, 1988.

_____. "On the State, Democratization and Some Conceptual Problems: Latin American View with Glances at Some Post-Communist Countries" *World Development* 21, no. 8 (1993).

O'Donnell, Guillermo, and Philippe Schmitter. *Transitions from Authoritarian Rule: Tentative Conclusions about Uncertain Democracies.* Baltimore: Johns Hopkins University Press, 1986.

Olsen, Mancur. *The Logic of Collective Action.* Cambridge: Harvard University Press, 1965.

Onis, Ziya. "The Logic of Developmental State." *Comparative Politics* (October 1991):124.

Organski, A.F.K. *World Politics.* New York: Knopf, 1958.

Ou-yang, Jen. "ROC's Constitutional Reform, 1990–1992." Master's thesis, National Chengchi University, 1994.

Palma, Giuseppe Di. *To Craft Democracies.* Berkeley: University of California Press, 1990.

Pang, Chien-kuo. *The State and Economic Transformation.* New York: Garland Publishing, 1992.

Pike, Fredrick, and Thomas Stritch, eds. *The New Corporatism.* Notre Dame: University of Notre Dame Press, 1974.

Przeworski, Adam. *Democracy and the Market.* Cambridge: Cambridge University Press, 1991.

Relations Across the Taiwan Straits. Taipei: Mainland Affairs Council, 1994.

Rigger, Shelley. "The Impact of Institutional Reform on Electoral Behavior in Taiwan." Paper delivered at the annual meeting of the American Political Science Association, Washington, D.C., 1993.

Robson, Peter. *The Economics of International Integration.* London: George Allen and Unwin, 1984.

Rosenberg, Gerald. *The Hollow Hope: Can Court Bring About Social Change?* Chicago: University of Chicago Press, 1991.

Ruseschemeyer, Dietrick, Evelyne Huber Stephens, and John Stephens. *Capitalist Development and Democracy.* Chicago: University of Chicago Press, 1992.

Rustow, Dankwart, and Kenneth Erickson, eds. *Comparative Political Dynamics.* New York: HarperCollins, 1991.

Samuels, Richard. *The Business of the Japanese State.* Ithaca: Cornell University Press, 1988.

Scalapino, Robert, Seizaburo Sato, and Jusfu Wanandi, eds. *Asian Economic Development—Present and Future.* Berkeley: Institute of Asian Studies, University of California, 1985.

Scherer, F. M. *Industrial Market Structure and Economic Performance.* New York: Rand McNally, 1980.

Shin, Doh Chull. "On the Third Wave of Democratization." *World Politics* 47, no. 1 (October 1994):135–170.

Simon, Denis Fred, and Michael Y. M. Kau, eds. *Taiwan: Beyond the Economic Miracle.* New York: M. E. Sharpe, 1992.

Skocpol, Theda. *States and Social Revolution.* Cambridge: Cambridge University Press, 1979.

Sornarajah, M. "Protection of Foreign Investment in the Asia-Pacific Economic Cooperation Region." *Journal of World Trade* 29, no. 2 (April 1995):105–129.

Stepan, Alfred. *Rethinking Military Politics: Brazil and the Southern Cone.* Princeton: Princeton University Press, 1988.

_____. *The State and Society: Peru in Comparative Perspective.* Princeton: Princeton University Press, 1978.

Stubbs, Richard. "Asia-Pacific Regionalization and the Global Economy." *Asian Survey* 35, no. 9 (September 1995):785–797.

Taiwan zhuquan xuanyan (Declaration of Taiwan's independent sovereignty). Taipei: DPP Headquarters, August, 1994.

Tien, Hung-mao. *The Great Transition: Political and Social Change in the Republic of China.* Stanford: Stanford University Press, 1989.

_____. "Taiwan's Parliamentary Election and Cabinet Reshuffling." Paper delivered at the Sino-American Conference on Contemporary China, Washington D.C., June 20–22, 1993.

Tsou, Tu-chi. "Party-State Relations in Taiwan." Ph.D. diss., National Chengchi University, 1993.

Tu, Wei-ming, ed. *The Confucian World Observed: A Contemporary Discussion of Confucian Humanism in East Asia.* Honolulu: Institute of Culture and Communication, The East-West Center, 1992.

Wade, Robert. *Governing the Market.* Princeton: Princeton University Press, 1990.

Wang, Li-hsin. *Wukui—Hao bocun di zhengzhi zhi lu* (Political Life of Hau Peitsun). Taipei: Tien Hsia, 1994.

Wang, N. T., ed. *Taiwan's Enterprises in Global Perspective.* New York: M. E. Sharpe, 1992.

Weber, Max. *Economy and Society.* New York: Bedminster Press, 1968.

_____. *From Max Weber: Essays in Sociology.* Translated and edited with an introduction by H. H. Gerth and C. Wright Mills. New York: Oxford University Press, 1958.

Weidenbaum, Murray. *Business and Government in the Global Marketplace.* Englewood Cliffs, N.J.: Prentice Hall, 1995.

Weidenbaum, Murray. "Greater China," *Vital Speeches*, December 1, 1993.

Wen, Hsin-ying. *Jingji qijide beihou* (Behind the Economic Miracle). Taipei: Independence Evening News Press, 1980.

Wiarda, Howard, ed. *New Directions in Comparative Politics.* Boulder: Westview Press, 1985.

Winckler, Edwin, and Susan Greenhalgh, eds. *Contending Approaches to the Political Economy of Taiwan.* New York: M. E. Sharpe, 1988.

Wu, Hsin-hsing. *Reaching Across the Strait: Taiwan, China, and the Prospects for Unification.* Hong Kong: Oxford University Press, 1994.

Wu, Jaushieh Joseph. *Taiwan's Democratization: Forces Behind the New Momentum.* Hong Kong: Oxford University Press, 1995.

Wu, Yu-shan. *Comparative Economic Transformation: Mainland China, Hungary, the Soviet Union, and Taiwan.* Stanford: Stanford University Press, 1994.

_____. "Mainland China's Economic Policy Toward Taiwan: Economic Reform vs. Unification." Paper delivered at the 23rd Sino-American Conference, Taipei, Taiwan, June 6–9, 1994.

Xu, Ze. *Li Denghui pingzhuan* (A Critical Biography of Lee Teng-hui). Hong Kong: Hsuan-huang, 1988.

Yeh, Milton D. "Ask a Tiger for Its Hide? Taiwan's Approaches to the Economic Transactions Across the Straits." Unpublished manuscript, 1994.

Yin, Robert K. *Case Study Research.* Newbury Park : Sage, 1989.

Zhonggong duitai yongwu kenengxingzhi fenxi (On the Possibility of the PRC's Using Force against Taiwan). Taipei: Government Information Office, 1992.

Zysman, John. *Governments, Markets, and Growth.* Ithaca: Cornell University Press, 1983.

About the Book and Author

Exploring the transitional role of the state in Taiwan's economic development, this book focuses especially on the impact of trade with mainland China. Tse-Kang Leng argues that the basic structure of political forces within Taiwan and its pattern of external economic relations have been transformed in the 1990s, with cross-Straits trade playing a key part. Although politically embarrassing to the government, this trade provides an economic opportunity that is irresistibly attractive to business interests.

Thus, cross-Straits trade and investment have served as a fulcrum by which societal interests have moved an unwilling state. Going beyond the "strong state" paradigm, the author's analysis of current cross-Straits economic policies reveals a sharp contrast between Taiwan's authoritarian past and its current era of democratization. Weighing the crucial forces at work in Taiwan—democratization, state-society interaction, and economic interdependence with mainland China—Leng provides a thorough analysis of Taiwan's political and economic development in the 1990s and beyond.

Tse-Kang Leng is an associate research fellow and chief of the Cooperation and Exchange Section of the Institute of International Relations at National Chengchi University, Taipei.

Index